The Third Key
A Study in Praise and Worship

Alvin Fruga

The Third Key: A Study in Praise and Worship

Copyright © 2017 by Alvin Fruga

All rights reserved. This book or any portion thereof may not be reproduced or used in any manner whatsoever without the express written permission of the publisher or Author except for the use of brief quotations in a book review.

Printed in the United States of America

First Printing, 2017

ISBN 978-0-9976124-8-6

Winters Publishing Group
2448 E. 81st Suite 5900
Tulsa, Ok 74137
www.winterspublishinggroup.com

Unless otherwise indicated, all Scripture quotations are taken from the *King James Version* of the Bible.

Scripture quotations marked *NASB* are taken from the *New American Standard Bible*®, © 1960, 1962, 1963, 1968, 1971, 1972, 1973, 1975, 1977, 1995 by The Lockman Foundation. Used by permission. (www.Lockman.org)

Scripture quotations marked *NIV* are taken from the *HOLY BIBLE, NEW INTERNATIONAL VERSION*®® 1973, 1978, 1984, 2011 by Biblica, Inc. ® Used by permission. All rights reserved worldwide

Scripture quotations market *NKJV* are taken from the *New King James Version*® © 1982 by Thomas Nelson. Used by permission. All rights reserved.

Contents

Dedication 4

Acknowledgements 5

Foreword 6

Chapter 1: *The Show Must Go On!* 11

Chapter 2: *We Were Created to Worship God* 25

Chapter 3: *That's Not Praise and Worship* 43

Chapter 4: *Now That's Praise and Worship!* 53

Chapter 5: *The Third Key* 75

Chapter 6: *Let's Bring the Presence Back* 95

Dedication

I dedicate this book to my precious wife, Sennola. You have been my wife for 31 years, and my very best friend for 49 years. What a journey! Love you, Babe!

Acknowledgements

I want to thank Tom Winters, Bryan Norris, Debby Boyd and the entire team at Winters Publishing for believing in what we have to say to the world, and partnering with us.

Special thanks to Ronald and Edna Jordan, owners of Jordan Media Services, for their editing support, and for being such great friends.

To Bishop Joseph and Lady Maddaline Norfleet for their spiritual oversight and friendship. What a tremendous blessing you both are to Sennola and me.

To our Presence Theater Church family in Owasso, Oklahoma, for their continued prayers and support.

To all of our family, including siblings, children, grandchildren and extended family.

A special thanks to Floyd and Momma Essie Mixon, the family patriarchs who continue to be a godly example to us all.

Foreword

Random thoughts of a worship leader on a Friday afternoon:

Don't forget to give the song list to Vicki to send to the worship team: two fast songs, two slow ones. I hope the church likes the new song. We've been rehearsing for months, trying to get it ready. Quite frankly, we still don't have it down, but we're going to give it a shot anyway. At some point, I just need to accept the fact that Kevin will never get that drum fill between the bridge and last chorus. I hope everybody shows up on time for pre-service rehearsal. We're really going to need it. God, I hope this doesn't turn into a train wreck!

Remember to tell Sam, for the hundredth time, that the lights go UP during praise and DOWN during worship—not vice versa! And what do I have to do to get the praise team to smile? I mean, is God REALLY their Friend or not?

I hope the congregation really gets in to the service Sunday. Sometimes I just want to stop right in the middle of the song and tell all the people with folded arms and sour faces to go home! We work too hard for them to stand there looking like zombies—like someone forced them to come to church!

Then there are the people who go just a little too far in their expression. How many times do I have to tell people that we don't have a dance ministry, so they can stop trying to audition during service? And how hard is it for the ushers to remember to confiscate tambourines at the door? Then there's

> Mrs. Brown, who screams, "Hallelujah," three times right in the middle of our last worship song. It scared me to death and almost gave poor, old Mr. Stanley a heart attack!
>
> Lord, if You could please help me make it through this weekend, I would truly be grateful. I promise to spend more time with You next week. I just need to get past this busy time of the year. Thank You for the challenge You have given me to lead Your people in worship every Sunday.

While these random thoughts may have made you chuckle a bit, or brought a smile to your face, I truly pray it is not reflective in any way of your life as a worship leader, music team member or lay church person. The sad truth is, most people who are familiar with the phrase *praise and worship*, usually think of it only in terms of the approximately 20 to 30 minutes that begin most church services.

Therein lies the purpose for this book.

As a worship leader, I have led praise and worship for many years in countless churches and other venues across the United States and in other parts of the world. I would like to say I have seen it all but the truth is, even after more than 25 years of serving in this area of ministry, there are still some things I haven't seen. There are limitless forms of expression, styles, stanzas and instruments which we use to tell God how much we love Him; how much we appreciate His kindness toward us; how glad we are to be part of His family.

Think, for a moment, about God's goodness in your life up to this point. No doubt, the simple realization of just how good He has been causes you to want to give Him thanks. It's not hard to find a reason to praise God, because as you think back, I'm sure you recall many times that He demonstrated His love to you. He is a merciful God, whose mercies are new every morning. His faithfulness is immeasurable.

So, if His goodness toward us is so great, His mercies extend to eternity, and His faithfulness is everlasting, how is it that we can fit our praise, adoration, thanksgiving and worship of such a great God into a brief, 20-minute slot once a week?

The truth is, we can't. So, we shouldn't even try.

Instead, we must put into action the mantra of the psalmist David, who said in Psalm 34:1, "I will bless the Lord at all times: His praise shall continually be in my mouth."

Notice what David said: "His praise shall continually be in my mouth."

There's a message in those few words if we will only take a moment and listen.

I believe what David was really trying to express was that there are really not enough days in our lifetime to sufficiently thank God for who He is and all He has done for us. I fondly recall the words of the old Pentecostal saints, who used to say: "If I had a thousand tongues I couldn't thank Him enough." I believe we do God a grave disservice when we think of praise and worship only in terms of what we do in a brief span of time during church service.

The truth is, praise and worship is not something *we do*. It is *who we are*.

The thing I love most about expressing my worship to God is that it never, ever gets old. Every time we enter that place of His presence, it's like the very first time; and yet we have a distinct feeling of déjà vu—like we are returning to a place we have been before. It's a place called *eternity*.

The presence of God is our natural habitat, and worship is our native language.

God's presence is eternal because He is eternal. And when we connect with Him on that level, whether in our car, office or church service, time ceases to exist and suddenly nothing else matters. In that moment there is absolutely no other place we would rather be.

Over the years, I have been privileged to visit some of the most beautiful cities and countries, enjoy the comfort of some of the nicest hotels, view numerous historic monuments, and enjoy the amenities offered by some of the most respected beaches and golf courses. But in all honesty, I don't believe the excitement and joy of anything I have ever experienced on earth can ever compare to the joy I feel when I enter that place God takes me in His presence. And there is absolutely no way I could be satisfied if it happened just once a week—if I had to wait until the next weekend service to have that experience.

Because I am a worship leader, I see the worship experience from a different vantage point than most. If you are a worship leader, praise singer or band member, you can relate to this. I get to see people as they worship God in a service. When I am leading, I get to see how exuberant or not people are when they praise, how heartfelt or not they are in worship, and their expressions, whether they are sincere or scream, "I can't wait until this is over."

Yes, I have seen people fold their arms instead of clap their hands. Others will keep their mouths shut refusing to sing, while some will even sit down when everyone else is standing. I have come to the conclusion that there are many people who simply don't understanding what praise and worship is all about. My prayer is that after reading this book you will not be one of those people, and that you will experience a newfound freedom in your praise, and a deeper level of intimacy in your worship seven days a week.

Chapter 1
The Show Must Go On!

"And out of the throne proceeded lightnings and thunderings and voices."
—**Revelation 4:5**

Have you ever wondered what worship is like in heaven? I have. Though I have not yet seen an actual vision of heaven, I have heard many firsthand stories from people who have experienced some type of vision or spiritual excursion to heaven. Many of these stories immediately bore witness in my spirit.

When you hear someone as they describe what their heavenly experience was like, it's almost as if they are describing, in great detail, the place where you were born and raised as a child. At some point, as you continue to listen to their account, you want to burst out and say, "Yes, that's where I'm from!"

One pastor described to me a vision he had of heaven. He saw in a distance a great mountain that was illuminated by a great light. He heard a sound coming from the other side of the mountain that was like nothing he had ever heard before. The sound was so wonderful, he said, that it was difficult for him to describe. The rhythm, along with the multitude of voices singing together, was incredible.

His story reminded me of Revelation 5:9:

> And they sung a new song, saying, Thou art worthy to take the book, and to open the seals thereof: for thou wast slain, and hast redeemed us to God by thy blood out of every kindred, and tongue, and people, and nation.

I believe it is important that we at least consider what worship is like in heaven. Because, quite possibly, *the way* worship takes place in heaven is *the way* that most pleases God. Our worship here on earth should be as close to "as it is in heaven" as possible (Matthew 6:10). The only way to accomplish that is to discover what's in God's heart concerning worship: what pleases Him.

God Enjoys a Good Show

As we take a closer look at Scripture, one of the first things we see is that God enjoys and appreciates a good show. That's right! God, the King of kings and Lord of lords, enjoys a good show. Have you ever wondered why God took six days to complete Creation? Couldn't He have accomplished it in a moment in time—or in the twinkling of an eye, just by speaking? Sure He could have. But that's not how God chose to fashion what would become one of His greatest works. I say "one" because no one knows for sure that God stopped there. He's God, so of course He could have.

There are possibly a number of reasons why God chose to spread Creation out over six days. Maybe He wanted to show us how to plan a project, and bring structure and order to our lives. Just read the book of Genesis and you can see He is for sure the God of order. The fact that He created everything in an orderly fashion is proof that He is the God of structure. Before He created the fowl of the air, for instance, He created the heavens. And before there were fish, He created the waters for them to swim in.

Or, maybe He wanted to teach us the importance of getting proper rest after completing a major project. That's what He did: "And on the seventh day God ended his work which he had made; and he rested on the seventh day from all his work which he had made" (Genesis 2:2).

While these are all legitimate reasons, I see another truth in the account of Creation. I believe God wanted to put on the most elaborate production ever witnessed by…well, Himself. This was a production that couldn't be accomplished or presented adequately in just one day. No. One day would not do it justice. Creation wasn't some quiet, humdrum event. It was a six-act production on the stage of eternity, with lights, music and a spectacle that will never be seen again until His return.

There's no way Creation was a quiet event.

I don't envision it that way.

I believe there was theme music, sound effects, angels flying and a light show for the ages. It would make the best Broadway or Las Vegas production look like an elementary school play. That's because anything God does is extraordinary and, well…*out of this world.*

There's a story in Judges that I believe provides us with a glimpse of heaven's showmanship. In Judges 13, an angel appeared to Manoah and his wife, who were the eventual parents of Sampson. Read what it says in verses 19 and 20:

> So Manoah took the young goat with the grain offering and offered it on the rock to the Lord, and He [the angel] performed wonders while Manoah and his wife looked on. For it came about when the flame went up from the altar toward heaven, that the angel of the Lord ascended in the flame of the altar. When Manoah and his wife saw this, they fell on their faces to the ground *(NASB)*.

How's that for a heavenly show?

Each time the flames flared up high toward the sky, the angel would shoot up toward heaven in the flames. This was such an amazingly breathtaking display that all Manoah and his wife could do was bow down and worship. No doubt, this angel was not doing this for the first time, but was quite possibly giving us a glimpse of the spectacle of worship that takes place in heaven.

Here's a news flash! Heaven is not a quiet place. Nor is it drab and conservatively decorated. Heaven really is an indescribable place in every way. Even if we combined the spectacle of lights from the Las Vegas strip with those of Times Square in New York, sprinkled in a sea of gold and crystal structures, and then added to all this some music and singing that was, well…*out of this world,* we still would not come close to adequately describing the look, sound and feel of heaven.

Speaking of gold, I am an alumnus of Oral Roberts University in Tulsa, Oklahoma. There are plenty of beautiful college campuses across the United State and around the world, but if you have never seen the campus of ORU in person you should. It is literally a sight to be seen! It is *out of this world.*

When you see this beautiful campus for the first time, it almost takes your breath away. Most people who see it for the first time generally have the same response: Wow!

The majority of the buildings have a gold mirror facade, which gives the grounds a rich look and feel that is unlike any other campus I have ever seen. As you drive up to this incredible place, there is a part of you that can't help but think, *I wonder if heaven looks anything like this?*

But as beautiful and ornate as the campus of Oral Roberts University is, it doesn't even begin to compare with what heaven looks like. Think of the most beautiful place you have ever visited. Think of the best concert you have ever attended. Do you remember how your senses began to do a dance? How you couldn't contain yourself or put into words what you saw, heard and felt? Well, my friend, heaven makes all that look and sound like a Saturday morning cartoon.

Revelation 4:8-11 says,

> And the four beasts had each of them six wings about him; and they were full of eyes within: and they rest not day and night, saying, Holy, holy, holy, Lord God Almighty, which was, and is, and is to come. And when those beasts give glory and honour and thanks to him that sat on the throne, who liveth for ever and

> ever, the four and twenty elders fall down before him that sat on the throne, and worship him that liveth for ever and ever, and cast their crowns before the throne, saying, Thou art worthy, O Lord, to receive glory and honour and power: for thou hast created all things, and for thy pleasure they are and were created.

Notice in verse 8 that worship before God's throne goes on nonstop, day and night. This must truly be some awesome worship, because it is contagious. Verses 9 and 10 say that when the four beasts worshipped, the other elders began to worship is well. And verse 11 concludes by saying, "and for thy pleasure they are and were created." The angels and creatures, in all their glory and spectacular ability to worship God in such a grandiose way, were created for just that specific purpose: to bring pleasure to God through the most creative expression that heaven can muster. Why? Because God enjoys a good show!

Presence Theater

My wife, Sennola, and I have attended many stage productions, both in New York and Las Vegas. We've seen a few shows on Broadway, including *The Lion King* and at least three performances of *Cirque du Soleil*. All these productions are top-notch with great singers, dancers, choreographed performers and awesome music. They represent some of the best entertainment one could experience.

While attending these productions, there was one question that always filled my heart. It's as though God were asking me: "Why doesn't My Church do this for Me?" One only has to attend one Broadway or Vegas show to realize they spare no expense in presenting the absolutely best production possible. These productions are so good that they demand top dollar. And we gladly pay it! The creativity that goes into producing these shows is so amazing and exciting that it causes your senses to fire on all cylinders.

The stage performers and musicians are very well-trained,

working in tandem to present their audience a show for their pleasure and enjoyment.

Again, I hear God asking, "Why doesn't My Church do this for Me?"

I'm certainly not being critical, but in most of our churches today, the praise and worship typically consists of two up-tempo songs, two worship songs and a prayer. For the average church, very little thought and creativity is given to how the worship will be presented to God.

Again, ponder the question I proposed at the beginning of this chapter: What is worship like in heaven?

Now, consider these questions:

If heaven is our example, is the worship in our churches anywhere close to being a reflection of what takes place in heaven? Is it possible that we are shortchanging God in our worship services? Are we falling short of the glory of God? Shouldn't our worship be of an even better caliber than those presentations on Broadway or in Las Vegas? Isn't God deserving of the absolute best? If we are not giving God our best, why aren't we? If God really does enjoy a good "show," why aren't we doing our best to give Him the "absolute best performance" we can offer?

Some may say, "Well, Pastor Alvin, the reason the secular world can put on these elaborate and grandiose productions is because they have the resources." While I agree with this line of thinking, I don't believe this is a good enough excuse for churches to take the "cheap route" on God's show. Every church has to get a vision for what it believes worship should look, and work toward that picture. While your vision may be to establish a 50-member team of singers, musicians and performers, you may have to start with only five.

"Why doesn't My Church do this for Me?"

I believe God asked me that to inspire me further into my purpose. That's one of the reasons the name of our church in Owasso, Oklahoma, is Presence Theater. Our tag line is, "A Place of Worship, An Audience of One." Our vision is to present the most elaborate worship, on the scale of a Broadway production, that is an awesome display of sight, sound and spirit. We're not quite there yet, but we're working on it. And someday, the word around Oklahoma will be, "If you get anywhere near Owasso you have to go see the worship at Presence Theater."

Remember, on earth as it is in heaven.

Author Michael Jinkins said it best in his book, *Letters to New Pastors*. He wrote: "Whether they are engaging in traditional, contemporary, or blended worship models, most of our churches deserve so much more than they're getting. I'm not arguing for liturgical elitism by arguing for depth. I'm simply pleading for our contemplation and worship of God to correspond to the awesome majesty and wonder of the God we worship."

When he says that most churches deserve so much more than they're getting, I totally agree. However, I would also add that our heavenly Father deserves much more than He's getting. What about what we as the Church are giving Him?

First Chronicles 29:1 says, "...for the temple is not for man, but for the Lord God."

Please highlight and underline this next statement.

Church is primarily for God. It's not for us.

Did you get that?

Church is primarily for God. IT IS NOT FOR US!

The enjoyment and enrichment we receive from going to church is merely the residue of that primary purpose.

You know that feeling you get when you're preparing to give someone a gift? You've gone shopping, found that perfect gift and wrapped it, all the while thinking about how much pleasure it's going to bring the recipient. They're going to love it! That's very similar to what it's like to go to church. We go to give God our gifts of worship, and the joy we receive is in knowing that God is really going to be pleased with what we bring Him.

I go to church because I want to present my gifts of worship to God. And I can't wait to see how He is going to respond to my gifts.

His response is always extraordinary. We receive joy unspeakable, and a peace that passes all understanding. But we came, first and foremost, to give to Him. When we move too far away from this primary purpose, we miss the true meaning of what we call "church."

Sure, there are many things we receive when going to church. We enjoy fellowship with our brothers and sisters in Christ. We receive biblical teaching and inspirational encouragement to help us make it through the week. We receive prayer for our needs. All these are good and needed, but they are not our primary purpose for going to church. We go for God's pleasure. Remember, it is the house of the Lord, not the house of the people.

Sadly, it seems that over the years the scale has tipped drastically toward what *we* want and need as opposed to what God desires. Church should have much more to do with what we give than it does with what we receive.

Think about the birth of Christ.

As recorded in Matthew 2, the Magi, who followed the star and came to Jesus, came bearing gifts. They came to give—not receive. They came, bowed down in worship and then presented their gifts to the Christ child. What these "wise men" did that day was a demonstration of church in its simplest and purest form.

I believe that, in many of our churches today, we have become so congregant-sensitive and program-driven that we have programmed God right out of the church. At the least, He is no longer the Guest of honor. We are more concerned with meeting people's needs than we are with how we can best honor God's presence. Many churches today have coffee bars, game rooms—even valet parking. And none of that is bad. But what we have lost in the process of striving to make everyone more comfortable with their church experience is our sensitivity and ability to give God the show He so deserves. God is still looking for His gold, frankincense and myrrh.

The second part of the statement we quoted earlier by Michael Jinkins, which really drives home the point concerning giving God our best, is the idea that our worship, in essence, should be a reflection of "the awesome majesty and wonder of the God we worship." When people see the worship in our churches, their response should be: "Wow! They must serve an awesome God, because they sure are going to great lengths to show it."

You can usually gauge how a person feels about you based on the type of gifts they give you. You can tell how much thought went into finding a gift they knew you would enjoy and appreciate. The value of the gift is also a factor.

In the same way, people can tell how much you love God based on your expressions of worship.

Jinkins' use of the phrase *awesome majesty* and the word *wonder*, scream spectacular display of Creation-like proportions. I believe the worship in our churches should be a celebration like no other, because we serve the God who is like no other. Our worship should be awesome, because He is awesome. Our worship should be majestic, because He is full of majesty. Our worship should be wonderful and glorious, because He is wonderful, and the whole earth is full of His glory.

When you think of worship in that way, the old tradition of four songs and a prayer just doesn't cut it. Honestly, while I'm sure God appreciates our effort, it wouldn't surprise me to know that He felt like He was being shortchanged.

"But Pastor Alvin, God doesn't look at the outward appearance, He looks at our hearts," you might say. And you're absolutely correct. The Bible is clear on that point in 1 Samuel 16:7: "But the Lord said unto Samuel, Look not on his countenance, or on the height of his stature; because I have refused him: for the Lord seeth not as man seeth; for man looketh on the outward appearance, but the Lord looketh on the heart." That's all the more reason to pull out all the stops, because our outward expression should be a reflection of our hearts.

So, how much do you love God? In your heart, I mean? And how do you express that love outwardly? To what extent are you willing to go to express all that is in your heart? Each service we attend should be considered a special appreciation service to honor and shower love on our King. How do you adequately honor and celebrate the King of kings and Lord of Lords? How do you do it in the most creative and expressive way? Can you ever go too far? Can you ever come to a place where you say "That's enough; He doesn't deserve all that"?

Let's ask the psalmist David. The Bible said he was a man with a heart after God (Acts 13:22), who danced with all his might when the Ark of God was being brought back to Jerusalem. Read how the Bible details David's elaborate procession in 2 Samuel 6:12-15, *NASB*, as he brings the Ark of God back into his city:

> Now it was told King David, saying, "The Lord has blessed the house of Obededom and all that belongs to him, on account of the ark of God." David went and brought up the ark of God from the house of Obededom into the city of David with gladness. And so it was, that when the bearers of the ark of the LORD had gone six paces, he sacrificed an ox and a fatling. And David was dancing before the LORD with all *his* might, and David was wearing a linen ephod. So David and all the house of Israel were bringing up the ark of the LORD with shouting and the sound of the trumpet.

The Show Must Go On!

David's first order of business when he became king of Israel was to bring the Ark of the Covenant back to Jerusalem. The Ark represented the very presence of God among Israel, and symbolized God's blessing and approval. After one disastrous attempt, which ended in a death, David regrouped and tried it again. This time he got it right.

Unlike the initial attempt, David followed proper protocol in transporting the Ark. It was carried with poles on the shoulders of Levites. The presence of God was to be carried "high and lifted up," the center of attraction for the entire world to see. This was a far cry from the first effort, where the Ark was placed on a rickety cart pulled by smelly oxen (see 2 Samuel 6). That's not the way you transport a king! He is to be raised up high—signifying that His power and authority are above all.

Remember Jesus' words in John 12:32? He said, "And I, if I be lifted up from the earth, will draw all men unto me."

The Church must get back to the primary purpose (the main thing) of "lifting up" Jesus in our services. David's procession of the Ark into Jerusalem was, for him, the main thing and it was like no other. Second Samuel 6:13 describes the process. Every six steps, David would stop the procession and sacrifice an ox and a fatted calf. This was a very involved process that took time. I'm not in the cattle business, and I've never slaughtered an animal. But my guess would be that it would take at least 45 minutes to kill and then sacrifice two animals. So, we could reasonably say that every six steps they stopped and had a 45-minute service. Let's look at it this way: Animal sacrifice is equivalent to our worship today. So, we could say that every six steps David stopped the procession and led the people in praise and worship. Every six steps they sang a new song unto the Lord. Needless to say, this was no quick procession.

Verse 14 goes on to say that David danced before the Lord (the Ark) "with all his might." Think what that must have looked like. Did David dance ballet? Was it modern dance? Was it hip-hop? Did he tap dance? Maybe it was a combination of all of these. One thing is for sure, David was exerting "all" the energy and effort he could muster because the verse says it was with "all his might" or physical strength.

The other thing we can say about David's dancing is that it was "before the Lord" in Spirit and in truth. He was not trying to be seen or draw attention to himself. He was genuinely expressing his joy for the Lord in a dance. Notice that God was not in any way displeased with David's dancing. Rather, He was displeased with David's wife who, because of David's dancing, "despised him in her heart." As a result of her criticism of David, the Bible says Michal, Saul's daughter, was barren until the day she died (see 2 Samuel 6:20-23). This is proof enough that dancing before the Lord is acceptable and pleasing to God when offered in the right spirit and with the right motives.

Verse 15 proves that David's elaborate production of bringing back the Ark of the Covenant was no quiet procession. There were shouts of joy, as well as trumpets. Maybe that's why David wrote in Psalm 100:1- 2, "Make a joyful noise unto the Lord, all ye lands. Serve the Lord with gladness: Come before His presence with singing."

Notice here the phrase *with gladness*, which is the same phrase used in describing how David brought the Ark back to Jerusalem in 2 Samuel 6:12. I can almost picture a large band playing and marching in perfect synchronization. This could have been the first parade ever recorded. What a sight it must have been. People from all over Jerusalem came out to see this awesome sight. I believe that's why his wife, Michal, was so upset. In spite of the criticism from his wife, David was not shaken or deterred from giving God the praise He deserves. Second Samuel 6:16 says that he was "leaping and dancing before the Lord."

There is a misconception concerning exactly what Michal was upset about. In 2 Samuel 6:20, when she said David "uncovered himself," it didn't mean that he danced totally out of his clothes, fully exposing himself. In essence, it meant that he danced out of his outer garment or coat. That would be equivalent to a man's suit coat today or the outer robe that a priest would wear. So, don't worry, David wasn't naked!

Now in Michal's defense, David was the king of Israel. He was that country's equivalent to our president of the United States. What Michal was actually saying was that a king should not be acting that way in public. After all, dancing so hard and furiously that one comes out of his coat or outer robe is not the type of display we would expect to see from those who are held in such high esteem—who hold the highest office in the land.

That said, I also understand David's response to his wife in 2 Samuel 6:21:

And David said unto Michal, It was before the Lord, which

chose me before thy father, and before all his house, to appoint me ruler over the people of the Lord, over Israel: therefore will I play before the Lord.

David didn't care what she or anyone else thought about the way he praised God. He couldn't contain his excitement over bringing the presence of God back to Jerusalem. To paraphrase what David said, "The show must go on!" In other words, David said he would not hold back in giving God the praise He deserves.

There are times when you have to throw caution to the wind and go for it! Giving God the thanks and praise He deserves is one of those times. David's feeling was if he embarrassed himself or his wife, in front of all Israel, so what? It was for a worthy cause, and let me add, THE MOST WORTHY God. And, he would do it again.

David spared no expense in giving God a great show.

Do you know how costly it must have been to sacrifice an ox and cow every six paces? It was a well-thought-out production, all for the sole purpose of celebrating the King of kings and the Lord of lords.

Now that, my friend, is Presence Theater!

As we continue on this journey of discovering a new dimension of praise and worship, always remember that heaven is a place of great celebration, pomp and circumstance, as well as a depth of honor and reverence—all for the Creator of all things. It is like nothing you will ever see on this side of heaven. However, that doesn't mean we shouldn't try to get close. You can be assured that God appreciates when we at least try. He is looking for something on the earth that resembles that which is in heaven.

Remember, on earth…as it is in heaven.

Let's give God the show He is accustomed to receiving!

Chapter 2
We Were Created to Worship God

"Thou art worthy, O Lord, to receive glory and honour and power: for thou hast created all things, and for thy pleasure they are and were created."
—**Revelation 4:11**

Man's greatest calling and purpose in life is to worship God, his Creator. There are many things man can accomplish while on this earth, but there is no one act, or collection thereof, that could ever supersede the act of worshipping his God. Man can climb the highest mountains, attain great wealth, win championships and medals in sports, raise a family, and reach all the goals he has set in his life. But nothing compares to that moment when he connects with the Father in worship.

"Why am I here?"

Some of you could spend your entire life searching for the answer to this question. Well, let me save you a little time and maybe a lot of heartache. You are here to worship God. You are here to offer your gifts, your talents and your breath in worship to the Most High God. You often hear people say things like, "I want to leave my mark," or "I want to leave a legacy." The greatest legacy a person could ever leave on this earth is that they were a worshipper of Almighty God.

Revelation 4:11 says all things (including us) were created to bring God pleasure. So we were created, we are here for Him. How do we bring God pleasure? To answer that question we need to go back to the beginning. Genesis 1:26 says, "And God said, Let us make man in our image, after our likeness: and let them have dominion over the fish of the sea, and over the fowl of the air, and over the cattle, and over all the earth, and over every creeping thing that creepeth upon the earth."

Notice, the first thing God said was, "Let us make man in our image, after our likeness." Stop right there. Take a deep breath. Before you begin to digest the rest of that verse, please understand this important fact: We were created to look like God. We were created to be a reflection of Him. We were created to be God's offspring. This truth is so vitally important, because we tend to find our significance in what we do rather than in who we are. But God views us as most significant when we can find pleasure in just "being" who He made us to be: like Him.

An expression and reflection of God is who we are. The very breath of God blows through us. The essence of who God is, is who we are. How do we bring God pleasure? By simply "being" who He made us to be. Not by doing, but just being. We honor God simply by looking like Him. We honor God most when He can look at us and see a reflection of Himself.

A great example of this is the story of Noah in Genesis 6. Read verses 8 and 9:

> But Noah found favor in the eyes of the Lord. These are the generations of Noah: Noah was a just man and perfect in his generations, and Noah walked with God.

The word *walked* in verse 9 literally means "to bring again and again." I believe Noah brought God his life every day as an offering of worship. He presented his life daily to God, which is what Paul encourages us to do in Romans 12:1: "Therefore, I urge you, brothers and sisters, in view of God's mercy, to offer your bodies as a living sacrifice, holy and pleasing to God—this is your true and proper worship" *(NIV)*.

Noah walked with God every day. He brought his image and likeness to God every day. He brought God a reflection of Himself every day. He reminded God every day that He is an awesome Creator. This is the reason Noah found favor "in the eyes" of God, because when God looked at Noah He saw a man who was content in just being with his Maker.

Do you remember when you had young, innocent puppy love for someone as a teenager? You were content just being in the same room with that person. You didn't necessarily have to do or say anything, because being together was enough. That's the way God is with us. We are fearfully and wonderfully made in God's image (Psalm 139:14) to bring Him pleasure simply by being with Him.

To Be or Not to Be

As I write this chapter, I realize that simply being without doing is a hard concept to grasp. But all our doing is a reflection of who we are, and if we don't have a firm grasp on who we are, our doing will be somewhat skewed. The most telling and powerful part of man is his heart. Before we do anything, God wants our heart. Matthew 22:37-38 says, "Jesus said unto him, Thou shalt love the Lord thy God with all thy heart, and with all thy soul, and with all thy mind. This is the first and great commandment."

The greatest thing that we can ever be is lovers of our God who created us. Our most significant mission on earth is to honor God with our life, with our heart. Before we do anything, we must be who God made us to be. We are, first and foremost, lovers of God. Our most important expression of honor and praise is first to our Maker.

Psalm 71:8 tells us, "Let my mouth be filled with thy praise and with thy honour all the day." My mouth, my hands, my body—they were all created in God's image and likeness, to give Him praise and honor. Do you ever notice that when you ask someone to tell you about themselves, one of the first things they tell you is where they work? That's because people equate what they do to who they are. But that's not the case. No matter what we do for a living, we are first and foremost children of God, created in His image for His pleasure.

Before God told us to "be fruitful, and multiply, and replenish the earth, and subdue it" (Genesis 1:28), He told us who we are. We were created to be worshippers. God made us human "beings," not human "doings." A worshipper of God is who I am, not what I do. What happens if you are no longer able to use your hands or mouth, or an instrument to worship God? Do you then cease to be a worshipper? Your expressions of worship are exactly that: expressions of who you are. So, if I could no longer raise my hand or speak or play an instrument, that doesn't stop me from "being" a worshipper, because I look like God.

The truth is, before we ever express our worship outwardly, God has already discerned who we really are by looking at our heart. God looks at our heart, because He wants to know if we really look like Him. He wants to know if our heart is really a reflection, image and likeness of His heart. First Samuel 16:7 says, "…for man looketh on the outward appearance, but the Lord looketh on the heart."

I am a worshipper not because of what I do on the outside. I am a worshipper because of who I am on the inside. God made me that way.

> What shall I render to the Lord for all His benefits toward me? I will take up the cup of salvation, and call upon the name of the Lord. I will pay my vows to the Lord now in the presence of all His people (Psalm 116:12-14, *NKJV*.

When you really think about it, what do you have of value that you could offer to God for all He has done for you? Money? God doesn't need your money. Your church needs your money to advance His kingdom on earth, but God doesn't need your money. The only thing of value that we could ever offer Him is who we are: our image and likeness of Him. Being who God made us to be is the highest form of honor and worship, and reminds God of how good He looks. When we simply make ourselves available to Him, like Noah did, we look our best! Anything else we attempt to offer God as worship is a sad and feeble attempt to improve upon perfection.

I mentioned this briefly in Chapter 1, but allow me to unfold another truth from Matthew 2:11. When Jesus was born in Bethlehem, wise men came to see Him. Look closely at what these wise men did when they came into the presence of the King. Matthew 2:11 says,

> On coming to the house, they saw the child with his mother Mary, and they bowed down and worshiped him. Then they opened their treasures and presented him with gifts of gold, frankincense and myrrh (*NIV*).

Notice that the wise men entered the house, and then fell down and worshipped Jesus. The next word in this verse is "then." The definition of the word *then* is "after that, next and afterward." It signifies a new event. These wise men did two things. First, they bowed down and worshipped. After that, they presented their gifts. This process is very important to understand, because it helps us see that our gifts are not our worship.

Follow the wise men's progression; they entered into the house, fell down and worshipped, and then presented their gifts. Their gifts were not their worship. Their worship was their worship. Their gifts were presented after they first worshipped. Once again, their gifts were not their worship.

Our gifts, our talents, our money, are of no value to God unless they are preceded by worship. What we offer God outwardly is not important if we haven't first exposed our true heart to Him in worship. It is sad to say, but there are many people serving in churches, giving their time, giving their money and offering their talents, who think they are doing God a favor with their gifts. But they haven't first worshipped. Their argument is that what they do in the church IS their worship. But as I mentioned earlier, what if you could no longer play an instrument or all your money was depleted? Would you then cease to "be" a worshipper? Who would you "be" then? The greatest gift the wise men gave to Jesus was not the gold, frankincense and myrrh. It was their honor and adoration of the King of kings.

Your gifts are simply an outward expression of who you are. When you serve in church, give your money, play an instrument, clap your hands and sing, these are all reflections of your heart. All that you "do" in church is an outward sign of who you are to the core. And since God looks at our hearts, judging our motives and intent, before we ever "do" anything, He has already assessed whether we are really worshipping or not.

Those who struggle with outward expressions of praise and worship are suffering from an identity crisis, because if they truly knew who they were in Christ, created in the very image and likeness of Almighty God, then expressing that outwardly wouldn't be a difficult task.

This gives new meaning to what Jesus said when He observed people giving offerings in the Temple in Mark 12:41-44:

> And Jesus sat over against the treasury, and beheld how the people cast money into the treasury: and many that were rich cast in much. And there came a certain poor widow, and she threw in two mites, which make a farthing. And he called unto him his disciples, and saith unto them, Verily I say unto you, That this poor widow hath cast more in, than all they which have cast into the treasury: For all they did cast in of their abundance; but she of her want did cast in all that she had, even all her living.

Notice that Jesus was observing "how" the people were giving their money. In other words, He was discerning their hearts. To Jesus, the actual amount they gave was secondary to their motives behind the giving. Jesus' description of the rich was that they were giving out of their abundance, which means in their hearts it really wasn't a sacrifice, and they probably thought they were doing the church and God a favor. The gifts of these rich people dripped with pride, whereas the widow's gift was saturated with brokenness and a total dependence on God.

Before Jesus saw their gifts, He had already discerned their hearts. The rich people were, in a sense, tipping God. But this widow literally poured out her heart when she gave her offering. That's why Jesus said that she gave more than all the rich people. Her heart was rich. Her actual gift of two mites was a reflection of her heart. Before God sees what's in your wallet, He sees what's in your heart. Whether we are giving of our time, our talents or our gifts, God is always looking for a heart that most resembles His.

When we worship God with the right heart, we look the most like Him. And when we are most like God, it gives Him the most pleasure. God is looking to see if you look like Him. We try so hard to impress God, many times making life more difficult than it really needs to be. However, when we, in the simplest of ways, can just "be" from the heart, it makes God smile. When a child emulates his or her parents, it makes the parents proud beyond measure. In the same way, when we worship God, it emulates the essence of who He is, and it reminds Him that making us in His image and likeness was a great idea. Yes, when we worship God, we look the most like Him. When we worship, our spiritual mannerisms shine through, and people can tell right away who our Daddy is.

My youngest daughter, Shannon, is a chip off the "young" block. She's an adult now, but when she was a little girl, people used to say she was a spitting image of me with pony tails. Not only did she inherit my great looks (smile), but she also inherited my anointing to play the piano, write songs and lead worship. I remember the first time I saw her sing a song from the piano. It was like looking in the mirror. She had all my little mannerisms and movements down pat. After watching me over and over again, it came naturally for her. I couldn't have been more proud. Still am. And just like Shannon spent countless hours with me, the more time we spend in the presence of our Father, the more natural it becomes for us to be a reflection of Him.

Ephesians 6:2 says for children to honor their father and mother. There is no greater honor as a parent than to see your child emulating the essence, the core values and the talents you possess. God is never more proud than when we become who He created us to be. He is honored when He looks at our heart and sees a reflection of Himself.

For His Pleasure

Earlier in this chapter, I referenced Revelation 4:11, which says that all things were created for God's pleasure. In Genesis 1:1, it says God created both heaven and earth. Revelation 10:6 says, "…[God] who created heaven, and the things that therein are, and the earth, and the things that therein are, and the sea, and the things which are therein." And in Colossians 1:16, we read: "For by him were all things created, that are in heaven, and that are in earth, visible and invisible, whether they be thrones, or dominions, or principalities, or powers: all things were created by him, and for him."

These passages of Scripture help drive home the point that God created everything in the heavens and earth. This is significant to understand, because this truth also proves that God created Lucifer, or Satan.

Let's take a brief look at this most interesting creation of God.

In Ezekiel 28, God sends a word to the King of Tyre, who was apparently operating under the influence and spirit of Lucifer himself. Some scholars believe this is a message directly to Lucifer, based on the vivid description given of him in this passage. At the very least, God describes this king's actions as if he were Lucifer himself. In doing so, we get a glimpse of Lucifer's origin and purpose. Read what Ezekiel 28:12-15, *NIV*, says: "Son of man, take up a lament concerning the king of Tyre and say to him: 'This is what the Sovereign Lord says:

"You were the seal of perfection, full of wisdom and

perfect in beauty.
You were in Eden, the garden of God; every precious stone adorned you: carnelian, chrysolite and emerald, topaz, onyx and jasper, lapis lazuli, turquoise and beryl. Your settings and mountings were made of gold; on the day you were created they were prepared. You were anointed as a guardian cherub, for so I ordained you. You were on the holy mount of God; you walked among the fiery stones. You were blameless in your ways from the day you were created till wickedness was found in you.'"

There is one other interesting description of Lucifer in Isaiah 14:11-12, which says,

Thy pomp is brought down to the grave, and the noise of thy viols: the worm is spread under thee, and the worms cover thee. How art thou fallen from heaven, O Lucifer, son of the morning! how art thou cut down to the ground, which didst weaken the nations!

The word *viols* basically means any type of stringed instrument. Now, we have already established that God created everything. We also know that anything God creates is undeniably beautiful. (All you have to do is look in the mirror to confirm that fact.) So, we can further conclude that Lucifer was one of the most beautiful and ornate beings in all of heaven. God described Lucifer as being "perfect in beauty." He was also very musical. God created Lucifer for the express purpose of creating the worship atmosphere in heaven.

It really is hard to put into words just how beautiful Lucifer looked and sounded. In heaven, all other angels knew when Lucifer was coming, because they could see and hear him from eternities away. Based on Ezekiel 28:13, he was covered with every precious stone you could imagine. These precious stones were inset into his heavenly body. This is what the phrase *settings and mountings* means as described in that verse. So, what happens when light hits a flawless diamond? It shoots beautiful rays of light. In the same way, when the light of God's presence hit Lucifer, it created the most amazing heavenly laser light show.

Not only that, "the noise of thy viols" mentioned in Isaiah 14:11 means that Lucifer had strings interwoven into his body. He was a walking orchestra! He was the epitome of sight and sound worship, and was amazingly beautiful. He was the cherub that covereth, which quite possibly means he hovered over the throne of God. Lucifer, having been created a musical being, could have also had pipes, like those of a pipe organ. Whenever the breath of God would blow through his pipes, Lucifer would be lifted up above God's throne, creating the most extraordinary music, along with a rotating light-ball effect from the precious stones reflecting off the light of God. It was such an awesome demonstration of worship that we can only imagine it.

The breath of God blew, and Lucifer hovered over the throne of God. The light of God shined on Lucifer's stone-embedded body, and shot colorful beams of light all throughout heaven, reflecting the Most High's essence. In response to heaven's worship leader, all the other angels bowed down to worship the King of kings. The breath of God—Lucifer hovered; the Light of God—Lucifer shined. Lucifer hovered and slowly rotated, while releasing the music of heaven, shining in God's presence. Lucifer was created to set an atmosphere of worship in the heavens. God created this masterful being for the sole purpose of bringing Him pleasure.

As previously stated, there really are no words that can adequately describe how beautiful Lucifer looked and sounded. His only purpose was to create an atmosphere of worship in heaven. Until, as described in Ezekiel 28:15, iniquity or wickedness was found in his heart. When iniquity was found in his heart, Lucifer ceased to be what God had created him to be. God dismissed him from his duties. Jesus speaks of this moment in history in Luke 10:18, where He said, "I beheld Satan as lightning fall from heaven."

When that happened, heaven was without its main worship leader. Imagine that if you can. For that moment, heaven was quiet. I believe it was at that moment God spoke and said, "Let us make man in our image and in our likeness." Here is a very important and powerful truth: God created us to take the place of Lucifer. When God breathed life into us, it was the same breath that caused Lucifer to hover over the throne in heaven. It is God's breath that blows over our vocal strings, that creates the sound, speaking and singing that comes out of our mouths.

This puts verses 5 and 9 in 1 Peter 2 in a totally different light.

> Ye also, as lively stones, are built up a spiritual house, an holy priesthood, to offer up spiritual sacrifices, acceptable to God by Jesus Christ.... But ye are a chosen generation, a royal priesthood, an holy nation, a peculiar people; that ye should show forth the praises of him who hath called you out of darkness into his marvellous light.

We are not dead stones, but lively stones. There should be a brilliance about us that causes our lives to shine with the glory of God. Consider the word *stones* not only as bricks, but precious jewels like the ones that covered Lucifer. We are now the "lively stones" that God created to "show forth," or shine forth His praises. Our precious stone is our heart. When God's light shines on our heart, our life, in turn, shines for all the world to see. We are the ones who have been created specifically to produce a beautiful sound when we open our mouths in praise to God. We are the ones who must allow the presence of God to permeate our lives so we can shine on the world. That's what Jesus meant in Matthew 5:16 when He said, "Let your light so shine before men, that they may see your good works, and glorify your Father which is in heaven."

In verse 14, Jesus declares that we are the "light of the world." When we offer our praise to God, we shine brightly in the world. That is why God created us. The phrase *show forth* in 1 Peter 2:9 literally means to "make known by praising or proclaiming; to celebrate." We were created by God to make known His goodness to the world. We were created to celebrate His glory and majesty—to be on earth what Lucifer was in heaven.

We are now God's covering cherubs. He made man to create on earth the atmosphere that is in heaven. When we think of our earthly purpose in this light, as that of replacing Lucifer, it is very easy to understand why he hates man so much. Lucifer can't stand it when we praise God. That's why he will do anything he can to stop you from praising God. You see, every time you praise God, it reminds Lucifer (Satan) of what he used to do before he was thrown out of heaven. Talk about being fired. He's like the disgruntled employee who is mad at the person who got the promotion he thought he deserved. Every time we lift our hands in worship to our Creator, it gives Satan fits. He can't stand it when we fulfill our purpose.

First Peter 5:8 warns that we are to "be sober, be vigilant; because your adversary the devil, as a roaring lion, walketh about, seeking whom he may devour."

Satan wants to devour your praise, your worship, your purpose. He wants you to stop being who God created you to be. He wants to snuff out who you are in God completely—to put an end to your primary purpose and minimize your effectiveness on earth. But the only way he can do these things is to get you to stop praising God. Satan doesn't care how much money you make or how successful you are. Those things are really inconsequential to him. What he absolutely can't handle, though, is when you look like God. If I can use street vernacular for a moment, God and Lucifer used to be *tight*. You might say they were "buds." But somewhere along the line Lucifer got the big head. He got to thinking he was better than God. So, God kicked him out! He showed Lucifer who the real boss was!

Now God is tight with us—you and me. And Lucifer can't

stand the fact that he has to sit back and watch us connect with our Father in a way that he used to. He will do anything to stop us from praising God. He will use anything he can to try and distract us from our ultimate purpose.

To a point he has been successful, because the truth is there are many things we allow to distract us from praising God. I'm not talking necessarily about sin. They are just things that we have allowed to take precedence over our intimacy with God. That's why we have to learn to properly manage our lives so we are always in the neighborhood of our purpose. There's really nothing wrong with television, computers, the Internet, social media and the like. But it is the managing of these and other activities that the enemy sometimes uses to distract us from spending time with the Father.

It has been said that if heaven is our home, worship is our native language. That means we must be careful that we don't go too long without speaking our native language or we run the risk of forgetting it. We must look again into the eyes of our Father and see what is most important to Him. We must not fit God into our schedules, but instead make sure our lives are always available to Him. We must continually pray that we never lose our hunger and thirst for the presence of God, for it is in His presence that we are most fulfilled.

Like Lucifer, we were created to bring God pleasure. Every time we express our heart to God through songs of praise and worship, every time we lift our hands, every time our heart wells up with tears of adoration, we fulfill our purpose and give the enemy fits. We are walking, breathing creations of sight and sound worship. When we walk into a room, the atmosphere changes because we are carriers of God's presence. When we go to church, we bring the praise with us because that is our purpose. No one has to tell, coach or beg me to praise God when I go to church. That would be like begging me to breathe. When I go to church, I go ready to fulfill my purpose because I was created to worship God!

What Happened to Our Image?

If we were created in the image and likeness of God to worship Him, then why doesn't everyone fulfill that purpose? Well, let's first clarify exactly what the phrase "image and likeness" means. Do we have an actual physical body like God? Does God have a body, meaning arms, legs and eyes, etc.? There are many scriptures that mention "His hand", referring to the hand of God. We know that God hears us when we pray, which would suggest that He has ears. In Genesis 3:8 it mentions God "walking in the garden in the cool of the day", which would suggest that He has legs. But Psalm 61:4 says "Let me take refuge in the shelter of Your wings." Does this mean that God also has wings? Well, if this verse is speaking literally, then we must not be made in God's image, because we definitely don't have wings. All of these verses that make reference to God having a physical body are speaking figuratively rather than literally. John 4:24 says that "God is spirit," which means He doesn't have a physical body like man.

John 1:18 says "No one has seen God at any time…" But if you saw God, what do you think His Spirit would look like? Would His Spirit be in the form of our human bodies? If so, how big or tall would He be? The fact is the human mind is incapable of describing what God looks like, because He is beyond our capacity to understand. So, when God speaks to us and even reveals Himself to us, He uses language, descriptions and pictures that we can understand.

In Philippians 2:7 Paul describes Jesus coming to the earth and says that Jesus was "made in the likeness of men". He goes on to say in verse 8 that Jesus was "found in appearance as a man." So here's my question; if we were made in the "physical" image and likeness of God, why would Jesus have to come down to earth and be made in the likeness of men if He already had that likeness in Heaven? How could He be found in the appearance of a man if our appearance is already a physical replica of His?

So, what did God mean in Genesis 1:26 when He said "Let Us make man in Our image, according to Our likeness."? What does it really mean to be made in God's image?

First, we know that Adam was created a three-part being: body, soul and spirit. This is a likeness of God, who is also a three-part being: Father, Son and the Holy Spirit. First John 5:7 says, "…these three are one." So, just as God is a three-in-one being, we are three-in-one beings. We reflect the image of the godhead.

Further, I believe the "image and likeness" of God refers to that part of man which cannot be seen in the natural. Adam "resembled" the spiritual, intellectual and creative attributes of God. He was a mirror image of the life of God, the spirit of God; created in perfect health and not subject to death. The immaterial part of man, which you cannot see with your physical eyes, is what looks the most like God. God is Spirit, so we are spirit. God is light, so we are the light of the world. God is love, and we are commanded to reflect the love of God to the world. The most significant part of man is not his physical body. It is that immaterial part of man that contains the essence of who God is. This includes man's spirit, and his ability to love, create, invent, be inspired, and yes worship.

Our heart, not the physical one that beats but the spiritual heart of man, serves as our spiritual central nervous system and is a mirror image of God. We are creative because God is creative. We love because God is love. We have original ideas because God is always original. We are not monotonous beings, because God is not monotonous. When we see someone in need we have to help them, because that part of God is woven into us, and it won't let us rest until we help them.

Jesus said in Luke 10:27, *NIV*,

"Love the Lord your God with all your heart and with all your soul and with all your strength and with all your mind," and, "Love your neighbor as yourself."

Notice that none of what Jesus told us to love God with is physical. He told us to love God with the "image and likeness" of who God made us to be. God created us with the ability to love Him simply by being who He made us to be. Man is the only created being that has the ability to connect spiritually with his Maker. God made us, first and foremost, so that we could be with Him. He created us to worship.

Now, everything was great and eternal until sin entered the picture. Sin changed our original image and likeness. It interrupted our relationship and fellowship with God.

When Adam and Eve sinned, something about their appearance changed. The Bible says their eyes were opened. But that couldn't mean that prior to sinning they were blind, because in the Garden of Eden "the woman saw that the tree was good for food, and that it was pleasant to the eyes." Not only that, but "she took of the fruit thereof, and did eat, and gave also unto her husband with her; and he did eat" (Genesis 3:6).

What they did see for the first time was that there was something different about their appearance. That's why they covered themselves with fig leaves (Genesis 3:7). God noticed there was something drastically different as well. That's why He covered them even better with the skin of an animal. Later, God would send His only begotten Son to cover all of mankind.

We know this much: Adam and Eve were eternal earthly beings before they sinned, and after sinning they lost their eternity. When sin entered, death kicked in and everything about Adam and Eve began to change. Romans 6:23 says, "The wages of sin is death…." Sin ages you and drags you to the grave. I'm sure you have met someone who you knew was living in sin, and they looked tired and worn, and maybe 10 years or more older than their actual age. Sin sucks the life out of you, partly because you're doing things to your body that are against God's original plan, and against the laws of nature.

God sent His Son, Jesus, to give us back our original image and likeness. Romans 6:23 continues by saying, "but the gift of God is eternal life through Jesus Christ our Lord." Sometimes you just need an unexpected gift to rescue you from a difficult situation that you lack the power to overcome by yourself. God favored us even when we didn't deserve it. He paved the way for us to get our lives back. Those who are living in sin have had their lives stolen by the enemy, but through Jesus

Christ they can get their lives back. God's plan of salvation is to return us to our original place near Him, and our original image like Him, so that we can once again have fellowship with Him.

Second Corinthians 5:17-18 says, "Therefore if any man be in Christ, he is a new creature: old things are passed away; behold, all things are become new. And all things are of God, who hath reconciled us to himself by Jesus Christ, and hath given to us the ministry of reconciliation."

The term *new creature* denotes a "new being." God made us new so that we could return or be reconciled back to Him. He wants fellowship with us because that's what was lost when Adam and Eve sinned. He takes joy in us being, again, who He made us to be. God just wants us to "be" with Him.

Chapter 3
That's Not Praise and Worship

"…for the Lord seeth not as man seeth; for man looketh on the outward appearance, but the Lord looketh on the heart."
—1 Samuel 16:7

Praise and worship. Do you know what that is?

I would love to see one of those street reporters ask that question as people walk by. For that matter, I'd really be interested in the answers they would get if they asked that question of people as they are leaving church service.

There are many misconceptions about the term *praise and worship*. So, before we dive in to what praise and worship is, let's first discuss what praise and worship is not.

One of the major misconceptions of praise and worship is that it is something we do during a church service. We sing, we clap, we lift our hands and we dance. Yes, these are all actions that demonstrate our praise to God, but is this truly praise and worship? I have heard many people define praise and worship by using the seven most commonly known Hebrew words for praise. Here are those seven words, and their meanings:

1. **Halal** — To be clear, to shine, to boast, to show, to rave, celebrate, to be clamorously foolish
2. **Yadah** — The extended hand, to throw out the hand, therefore to worship with extended hands; to willfully throw your hands up to praise with power
3. **Todah** — From the same principle root word as Yadah,

but is used more specifically. Todah literally means an extension of the hand in adoration, avowal or acceptance.

4. Shabach — To shout, to address in a loud tone, to command, to triumph

5. Barak — To kneel down, to bless God as an act of adoration

6. Zamar — To pluck the strings of an instrument, to sing, to praise; a musical word which is largely involved with joyful expressions of music with musical instruments

7. Tehillah — Derived from the Hebrew word *halal*, and means the singing of halals, to sing or to laud; perceived to involve music, especially singing; hymns of the Spirit

These Hebrew definitions of praise and worship describe actions, or expressions—things we do. But I would submit to you that a more precise and accurate definition of praise and worship would not be so much in what we do as who we are.

Praise and worship is not about simply singing a song. Praise and worship cannot be defined simply as dancing, clapping or shouting out loud the goodness of God. In truth, praise and worship has absolutely nothing to do with music. Yes, you read it right. Read it again in bold print: **PRAISE AND WORSHIP HAS ABSOLUTELY NOTHING TO DO WITH MUSIC!**

How can I say this?

The psalmist David, who is considered one of the foremost biblical authorities in the area of praise and worship, asked God this question in Psalm 15:1:

> Lord, who shall abide in thy tabernacle? who shall
> dwell in thy holy hill?

Notice in this verse that David acknowledges God dwells in a high place. In the Old Testament, the presence of God was usually found on a mountain. For example, in Exodus 3, when Moses received the call from God to deliver the children of Israel from bondage in Egypt, it was on a mountain where a bush burned but was not consumed. Later, in Exodus 19, when Moses met with God to receive the Ten Commandments it was on a mountain. Verse 3 says, "And Moses went up unto God, and the Lord called unto him out of the mountain."

In every instance in the Bible where God met with man, He always required that they come "up" to where He was. Yes, He sent Jesus down to Earth to save us from our sins, but in response to this awesome demonstration of humility and sacrifice we have to "come up." Isaiah 30:18, *NASB*, says, "Therefore the Lord longs to be gracious to you, and therefore He waits on high to have compassion on you."

In light of this, we can view praise and worship as a journey up to the mountain of God to meet with Him. A great example of praise and worship is that of someone climbing or hiking to the top of a mountain. Once they reach the peak of the mountain, they are overtaken with a sense of accomplishment and satisfaction as they take in the moment and enjoy the incredible view. In terms of praise and worship, the reward for getting to the top of the mountain of God is the opportunity to meet with the Father. I'll talk more about this concept in the next chapter, but for now just know that if you are not getting to the top of the mountain in your praise and worship, you are really missing out on a spectacular view.

Man must go up in order to meet with God: up in his mind; up in his heart; up in his soul; and even up in his body. We must lay aside all distractions and elevate ourselves to meet with our God, who sits high and looks low. Man must make the decision to go up and see what God is all about. We understand that He is omnipresent, which means everywhere present. So, one might ask, "Why do I need to go up to Him if He is already here?" The fact is, He's here, but we're not. We are not where He is until we acknowledge Him. We are not where He is until we give Him our undivided attention. So, we must "go up" in our heart, mind and soul. God always calls those He wants to meet with "up" to where He is.

From his youth, David loved to sing and worship God. As a

young shepherd boy, he would spend countless hours underneath the stars, singing, writing songs and worshipping God while tending sheep. It was during these times that David learned to appreciate the awesome presence of God. On many occasions David ascended, not physically but spiritually, to the top of the mountain to meet with God. This was quite possibly the reason David was described as being "a man after God's own heart" (Acts 13:24).

I believe David's question in Psalm 15:1 was inspired by these precious moments he experienced in God's presence while he tended the sheep. It was like David was asking God, "Lord, who can come up to Your presence and worship You?"

Could anyone approach God's Tabernacle? Was it possible that anyone could dwell in His holy hill? Could anyone experience what David had experienced on many occasions? The answer is given in the very next verses.

> He who walks with integrity, and works righteousness, and speaks truth in his heart. He does not slander with his tongue, nor does evil to his neighbor, nor takes up a reproach against his friend (Psalm 15:2, 3 *NASB*).

Notice that the answer given here has nothing to do with music. It doesn't say, "He who sings two praise songs and one worship song." Or, "He who claps his hands, plays an instrument or dances before the Lord." God is obviously much more interested in the condition of your heart than He is the act of your worship. Before you ever sing or play a note, your heart must be in a place of complete surrender before God. Otherwise, your worship offering is blemished and unacceptable.

David asks a similar question in Psalm 24:3, *NASB*: "Who may ascend into the hill of the Lord? Or who may stand in His holy place?" Again, notice that the presence of God dwells in a high place that we must ascend to. The answer to David's question is very similar to the one in Psalm 15. It's just said in a different way. Verse 4 says, "He who has clean hands and a pure heart, who has not lifted up his soul to falsehood and has not sworn deceitfully" *(NASB)*.

Once again, God is showing us that He is much more concerned with our deeds (clean hands), and our motives (pure heart), than He is with our song. He desires, and even requires that our lives are reflective of the songs we sing. We must begin to view praise and worship from God's vantage point. He doesn't look at what we do as much as He looks at the heart in which we do it.

> For man looks at the outward appearance, but the Lord looks at the heart. (1 Samuel 16:7, *NASB*).

Therefore, praise and worship is more a matter of the heart, rather than of actions. Our actions, which can include singing, clapping, dancing, and shouting, should be a reflection of our heart. The seven Hebrew words for praise we discussed earlier are but empty and lifeless expressions without a submitted heart to God. Our hearts must be in the right place if God is to take pleasure in our acts of praise.

Don't Come Any Closer

In Exodus 3, we see Moses tending the flock of his father-in-law, Jethro—minding his own business when, suddenly, he looks up and sees a bush burning on a mountain. The crazy thing is that it took a while for Moses to realize that the bush was burning, but not being consumed by the fire.

He must have thought, *Hmm. Must be some special bush.*

Deciding he wants to go up and see what this burning bush is all about, and apparently recognizing that this must be an act of God, Moses drops what he is doing and turns his attention to what is burning on the mountain. At that moment, nothing is more important to him than seeing God.

There's a lesson here that we can learn from Moses' decision to act.

God wants our undivided attention, without any distractions. He wants us to drop what we are doing, rise above our situations and circumstances, and realize that He is way above all that we might be concerned about, distracted with or running from. Therefore, when He calls, like Moses, we must be willing to drop whatever we're doing and go up to experience the burn of God. That is the essence of praise and worship. Unfortunately, as with Moses, sometimes in our zeal we miss something.

In Exodus 3:5, *NLT*, as Moses got closer to the burning bush, God called out to him from the bush and said, "Do not come any closer." Why would God tell Moses not to come any closer? Doesn't He want His children to enjoy His presence? Doesn't He want us to come up to where He is and worship Him? After all, weren't we created to praise God?

As a young boy growing up in the church, I often got the impression that God was, for lack of a better word, *desperate* for us to praise Him, to the extent that He would accept anything we offered Him. Now, you may think that sounds a little odd, but that is another serious misconception of praise and worship today. Sometimes we praise God, while in our mind we are saying, *Well, I know this isn't my best, but He will accept it anyway.* We think God doesn't have any standards, but that couldn't be further from the truth.

Notice in verse 5 that God didn't say, "Hey Moses, come on up. I've been waiting for you to come up and acknowledge Me with your worship." No, even though He calls us, His invitation doesn't come without Kingdom standards. Even though He longs for us to worship Him, He doesn't accept just anything. When you order a meal at a restaurant, do you accept anything different than what you have ordered? In most cases, you would not. If the server brings you something you didn't order, likely you will send it back. Likewise, God has ordered His worship in a certain way, and if it is not delivered the way He ordered it He has every right to send it back and say, "Don't come any closer."

God required Moses to acknowledge that he was in the presence of the Almighty first, and also required him to face who he really was and what he had done. God said, and I paraphrase, "Moses, take off your shoes. You have killed in those shoes. You have run from your calling in those shoes. So, let's start fresh. Take off your past and we can get started with your future."

In biblical times, the shoes (actually sandals) a person wore revealed a lot about who they were as a person and their status in society. For example, a wealthy person often wore sandals made from badger's skin, which is softer than the wood or matted grass sandals that a shepherd might wear in the fields. It also wasn't uncommon for a poor person to have no sandals at all.

A person's sandals were also representative of their journey in life; where they had traveled, etc. If the shoes in your closet could talk, I wonder what they would say. If you know the story of Moses, you know his life was not without its hiccups. His journey included killing a man, and then running away when he learned that his crime had been witnessed. In fact, that was why Moses left Egypt and was tending Jethro's sheep. Isn't that a perfect example of God's grace and mercy? Even when we try to run from our destiny because of mistakes we have made, God still has a way of reaching us. Even when we are running away from God, we're actually running to Him.

What stories could your shoes tell about you? Not your actual shoes, but your transparency before God? What do you have on your shoes? What are you running from? I assure you there's nothing you have done or experienced that can cancel out God's ultimate plan for your life. All you have to do is be available. Like Moses, you simply have to be willing to drop what you're doing, go up to Him, and take off your shoes, being totally transparent before the Father.

Many times when we are approaching God's presence in worship, He calls out to us like He did to Moses and says, "Don't come any closer." God told Moses to take off His shoes because the area where he stood was holy ground.

What is God really saying to us through this account of Moses? If we want to go up to His presence, we have to be willing and ready to deal with the stuff on our shoes. If we want to experience God on a higher level, we must be willing to lay down who we are—the good, the bad and the ugly—fully exposing our lives to Him.

When I first began to study this story, a couple of things quickly came to mind. First, I remembered a sign I would occasionally see posted on the doors of businesses, particularly of stores and restaurants. The sign read: "No shoes. No shirt. No service." While this seems the opposite of taking off your shoes, the principal is the same. Businesses have set certain standards and requirements that customers must meet in order to purchase their goods or services. You must come properly dressed or you will not be served. I believe in the same way, God requires that we come "dressed" with the right heart. If not, He is under no obligation to serve our needs.

My mind also went back to my childhood, when my brothers and I would spend the hot summer days playing outside. We would eventually get thirsty and run inside the house to get a drink of cold water. Mom would hear the door slam, and the conversation would go something like this:

"Hey! What are you boys doing?"
"Getting some water."
"Use the faucet outside."
"That water is hot."
"OK, well, if you're going to come inside, take off your shoes."

Now, the reason our parents demanded that we take off our shoes was because they didn't want us trampling dirt into the house. As a little boy wanting to hurry up and get back outside to play, taking off my shoes was the last thing on my mind. It was an inconvenience! As a matter of fact, I remember thinking, *When I grow up and have kids, I'm not going to make my kids do this.*

Fast forward about 20 years.

You guessed it! As a parent, I made my kids take off their

shoes when they would come inside from playing.

God's presence is so awesome and precious. He doesn't want us to destroy the luster of His presence with dirt from "outside" any more than our parents wanted us to. God has standards, and we must be willing to take off our shoes, even lay down our lives, to experience all that He has burning for us. We must come with a completely yielded and transparent heart. If we're not willing to do that, then what we are doing is not truly praise and worship.

Chapter 4
Now *That's* Praise and Worship!

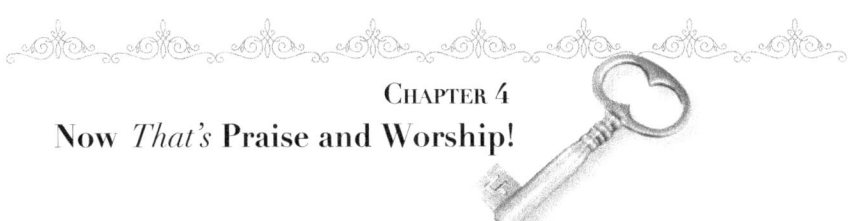

"The sacrifices of God are a broken spirit: a broken and a contrite heart, O God, thou wilt not despise."
—**Psalm 51:17**

I want to begin this chapter by sharing with you four principles that will reveal some of the foremost characteristics of praise and worship, and give us a better understanding of exactly what praise and worship is.

Principle No. 1: Praise and Worship Is a Godly Lifestyle

When we live in a way that is pleasing to God, that, in and of itself, is praise and worship. Our lives should be a beautiful song that rises to God as a sweet aroma in His nostrils and a sweet sound in His ears. A great example of this principle is found in Psalm 51. After David sinned with Bathsheba, he asked God for forgiveness. In Psalm 51:1-10 David acknowledges his sin and pleads with God to cleanse him. Read what David says:

> Be gracious to me, O God, according to Your lovingkindness; according to the greatness of Your compassion blot out my transgressions. Wash me thoroughly from my iniquity and cleanse me from my sin. For I know my transgressions, and my sin is ever before me. Against You, You only, I have sinned and done

what is evil in Your sight, so that You are justified when You speak and blameless when You judge. Behold, I was brought forth in iniquity, and in sin my mother conceived me. Behold, You desire truth in the innermost being, and in the hidden part You will make me know wisdom. Purify me with hyssop, and I shall be clean; wash me, and I shall be whiter than snow. Make me to hear joy and gladness, let the bones which You have broken rejoice. Hide Your face from my sins and blot out all my iniquities. Create in me a clean heart, O God, and renew a steadfast spirit within me *(NASB)*.

In verses 11 through 15, David acknowledges feeling separated from God, and begs Him to take this feeling away so he can once again sing forth His praises. David could not, in good conscience, worship God knowing that his life was unclean. In verse 16, *NASB*, he says, "For You do not delight in sacrifice, otherwise I would give it; You are not pleased with burnt offering." David knew if he was not in right-standing with God, the last thing God would delight in would be his worship. He continues in verse 17: "The sacrifices of God are a broken spirit; a broken and a contrite heart, O God, You will not despise."

The word *sacrifices* means an offering. In biblical times, a person's offering was a bullock, a goat or some other animal, which represented their form of worship to God. Today our sacrifices, what we offer to God, consist of our expressions of praise and worship. So, we could paraphrase verse 17 to read: "The praise and worship of God is a broken spirit; a broken and a contrite heart."

David knew he was in big-time trouble with God. He also knew God would not delight in his worship without first resolving this heart issue. In other words, God didn't want David's song if his heart wasn't right. The only song of praise and worship God wants is one of a broken spirit and a contrite heart that says, "God, I've done wrong. Please forgive me."

For too long, we have attempted to separate our worship from our lifestyle. This verse of Scripture makes clear the fact that before God ever hears your song, He sees your heart. And if your heart does not line up with the song, God cannot and will not delight in it. We mentioned Romans 12:1 in an earlier chapter, but it bears repeating here:

> Therefore I urge you, brethren, by the mercies of God, to present your bodies a living and holy sacrifice, acceptable to God, which is your spiritual service of worship *(NASB)*.

Our lives should be a living and holy song of worship to God. That is the only way they will be acceptable to Him. In reality, our praise and worship should be a mirror image of our heart. We cannot truly sing about that which our heart has not experienced, embraced or become. Our life, our very breath, is something we should present to God daily as worship. When we live our lives in a way that is pleasing to God, it's as if we are singing the most beautiful song of worship to Him. And that, David said, God will not despise or turn away from.

Do you really have a desire to worship God? If your answer is yes, you must learn how to worship God with your life.

Principle No. 2 — Praise and Worship Is Obedience to God

Let's say, for a moment, that it's Sunday morning and you are at home preparing to go to church. While brushing your teeth you get a "spiritual nudge," impressing you to call a friend to see if they need a ride to church. You say within yourself, "OK, they usually ride with another friend, but I'll call them as soon as I finish getting ready." You continue preparing for church and are ready to walk out the door when you get that "spiritual nudge" again. But now you're running a little late, so you decide to go on to church, telling yourself if your friend is not at church when you get there then you'll go pick them up. Yeah, right.

After arriving at church, you greet numerous people in the lobby on your way into the sanctuary. You hear the music playing and are excited about participating in worship. You rush in, clap your hands, start to sing and begin your trek to the presence of God. As you lift your hands in worship, there it is again: that "spiritual nudge" one more time. Yeah, that same nudge you received twice while at home getting ready for church. You look around to see if your friend is there, but the friend you were supposed to call is nowhere to be found. At that moment, how do you feel?

Those "spiritual nudges" could quite possibly have been God's way of telling you that your friend needed a ride to church. If that's the case, your unwillingness to respond to God's nudge could be considered disobedience. We all get those nudges from time to time. It's God's way of prompting us into good deeds of service. Too often, we are too busy focusing on the big stuff to recognize that God is just as concerned with small, random acts of kindness like a simple telephone call.

What does this have to do with praise and worship? Well, God responds to His children the same way we respond to ours. Who do you think we learned it from?

Here's another scenario.

Let's say you tell your child, niece or nephew to clean up their room. Later that day, they come to you and ask if they can go outside and play. In that moment, what is your response to their request? All together now...

"Did you clean up your room?"

If they answer yes, then you most likely will allow them to go outside and play. But if they did not clean their room, your response is going to be something like, "Go clean up your room first, then maybe you can go outside and play." There is no way you are going to allow them to go outside and play if they have not been obedient to what you asked of them. Our heavenly Father is the same with us when we express our desire to be in His presence. We lift our hands, close our eyes and say, "Take me away, God." No response. "Let's try this again," we say. We lift our hands while forcing a tear to roll down our face, as we say, "I love You, Jesus." Again, no response. Then we hear God clear His throat. We open one eye, hands still raised, and say, "Something wrong, God?" And He says, "Did you call your friend like I asked?" We drop our hands and lower our head and say, "No."

In that moment God has every right to say, "Well, go do what I asked you to do first, then come back and worship Me." But He doesn't. God doesn't completely reject us, but He does use these moments of weakness on our part to teach us obedience. And, yes, worship. As we discussed earlier about Moses at the burning bush, God didn't utterly reject Moses, but He did require him first to take off his shoes. The point is, we can't be disobedient to God, and then expect Him to receive us with open arms to enjoy the fullness of His presence. That was the whole idea of David's prayer in Psalm 51.

When God asks us to do something and we do it, we have just offered to God the most awesome song of praise and worship imaginable. How many times have we missed out on some great praise and worship simply because of our disobedience?

Hebrews 11:6, *NASB*, says, "And without faith it is impossible to please Him, for he who comes to God must believe that He is and that He is a rewarder of those who seek Him."

One of the Greek renderings for the word *faith*, as used in this verse, is "to obey." The idea here is that true faith is displayed through obedience. The evidence of your faith is your obedience. If you have unwavering faith in who someone is and what they say, you will have no issue with doing what they ask of you. Your obedience is proof that you have faith in them. So we could interpret Hebrews 11:6 in this way: "And without obedience it is impossible to please Him, for he who comes to God must first obey, knowing that He is God and that He is a rewarder of those who seek Him."

No matter how well you sing, play an instrument or dance, God will not be pleased if you have not first been obedient to Him. You cannot come to God with your praise and expect Him to embrace your offering if you have neglected His nudge. First Samuel 15:22, *NASB*, says, "Has the Lord as much delight in burnt offerings and sacrifices as in obeying the voice of the Lord? Behold, to obey is better than sacrifice, and to heed than the fat of rams."

Principle No. 3 — Praise and Worship Is an Outward Reflection of Your Inward Devotion

If you have a genuine love for God in your heart, then that love should be easily reflected outwardly in your expressions of praise and worship. Over the years, my ministry endeavors have given me the opportunity to travel quite a bit. During the early years of our ministry, when our children were much younger, my wife, Sennola, was not always able to travel with me. There were many times when I would be gone for a week or more. Whenever I would return home from one of these trips, long or short, there was never a time when I needed someone to call me and say, "Pastor Fruga, I am calling to remind you that you have been away from your wife for a week. I want to encourage you to show some love and affection to her right away."

My point is this: When you are truly in love with someone, you don't need anyone to coach you or remind you to show affection toward them. There is something on the inside of you that compels you to express what is in your heart. In the same way, if you truly love God, and you realize that you would be a total wreck without Him, no one should have to remind or prod you into expressing your love to Him. There should be something inside you that moves you and prompts you to praise God. It is not the responsibility of the worship leader to get you in the mood to praise God. An expression of praise should already be in your heart and readily on your lips when you go to church.

This is why I don't understand those people in church whom you have to pump up and almost beg to praise God. I question the inward devotion of someone who displays no outward affection toward God. As a worship leader for many years, I can't tell you the countless number of people whom I have witnessed being unresponsive to the presence of God during a service. It is almost as if someone threatened them, and made them go to church. Where is the inward devotion? Where is the love and passion for God? Oh, what great services we would have if everyone who came to church came with a passion and love for God, and was ready and willing to express it outwardly.

I enjoy expressing my love to my wife. Why? Because I am head over heels in love with her. There should always be a "why" to your praise. Why are you praising God? What has God done for you? What has He brought you out of or rescued you from? Where would you be if the Lord had not saved you? These are great questions to ask as you prepare to worship God, because they remind you of His goodness in your life. When you do this, I guarantee you will not have a problem displaying outward affection toward God.

Some years ago, I had the awesome opportunity of taking a trip to Israel. During this trip we visited the Dead Sea. The Dead Sea is like no other body of water in the world. At 1,400 feet below sea level, it has the Earth's lowest elevation on land. It is called the Dead Sea because of its high salt content, which prevents the existence of any life forms in it. In addition, because of its high salt content, the Dead Sea is 100 percent buoyant, meaning nothing is able to sink in this most unusual black-colored, murky body of water. Interestingly enough, the tour guide encouraged us to swim in the Dead Sea so we could see what it feels like to be in a body of water like that. I took the plunge and quickly realized that it, in fact, is a dead sea. I had someone take a picture of me in the water, floating on my back while easily reading a newspaper.

As I floated in this dead body of water, I was reminded of the scripture in Psalm 22:3 that says, "But thou art holy, O thou that inhabitest the praises of Israel."

As I was still floating in this mucky, thick body of salt water, I remember God speaking to my heart saying, *Alvin, this is sometimes how it feels when I come to dwell in the praises of My people.* God desires to dive in and dwell in our praises. He wants to enjoy all that we have to offer Him from our heart. But just like I couldn't stay submerged in the Dead Sea too long because of its condition, God many times doesn't want to linger in our praise and worship because of its condition.

Is your praise and worship like the Dead Sea? Is God displeased when He comes to dwell in your praise? I encourage you to examine your heart. Maybe it has become hard over the years. Maybe there is such a buildup of disappointments and hurts that your praise has no life or depth. If so, simply ask God to change the wineskin of your heart so that you can once again offer Him a true heart of worship—something that He would be pleased to dwell in.

Principle No. 4 — Praise and Worship Is Acceptable to God Only When Offered in Spirit and in Truth

John 4:23-24, *NASB*, says, "But an hour is coming, and now is, when the true worshipers will worship the Father in spirit and truth; for such people the Father seeks to be His worshipers. God is spirit, and those who worship Him must worship in spirit and truth."

First, to really understand the meaning of this text, we must define the words *spirit* and *truth*. The word *spirit* is taken from the Greek root *pneo*, which means "to breathe hard." It more broadly means, "God, Christ's spirit, the Holy Spirit and life."

The application of this definition can be found in the context of the story preceding these verses in John 4. In verse 7, a woman from Samaria came to draw water from a well. Jesus was there and asked for a drink from her, which resulted in a brief conversation between the two of them.

It was common knowledge that the Jews did not have any dealings with the Samaritans. Verse 20 further reveals that there was also a debate between the Jews and Samaritans over whether the correct location to worship God was on a nearby mountain or in Jerusalem. Jesus responds to this conflict in verse 21 by saying, "Woman, believe Me, an hour is coming when neither in this mountain nor in Jerusalem will you worship the Father" *(NASB)*.

Jesus was pointing out the truth that there is coming a time when it won't matter where you are located geographically, as long as you are connecting to the Father by His Spirit. He was saying that when we have tapped into God, through His Son, Jesus, and the Holy Spirit which He freely gives us, we can worship Him anywhere, as long as we are effectual and fervent in how we connect with Him. The phrase *effectual, fervent* (James 5:16) literally means "to breathe hard." This is true and passionate worship. Our worship should be with life, energy and passion, because there is nothing dead about God.

The word *truth* in John 4:23 is defined as "being real, and not concealed." It means "to be fully exposed." In Jesus' encounter with this Samaritan woman, after giving her the truth, she wants to drink of the water that Jesus offers. Jesus' reply basically inferred the following: You have to expose everything about yourself and come clean before you can partake of this water. In other words, we can't fully benefit from what Christ has for us unless we are first willing to admit that we have issues. We must be willing to bring our issues to God and fully expose them before His presence.

This type of truth should be demonstrated not only between God and man, but between man and his brother. How can we truthfully and openly worship God when we have an issue with our brother?

It is this type of "truth" between brothers that is the center point of the rift between Cain and Abel. In Genesis 4, Cain brought his offering to God, but God wasn't pleased with what he offered. Abel then brought his offering and God was pleased with what Abel offered. Cain got angry and jealous over God's pleasure with Abel's offering, and as a result killed his brother.

There is much that we can learn from this story about being truthful with God and our fellow man. First, I don't believe someone just ups and kills another person as a result of one isolated incident. No, I believe Cain had a long-standing issue with Abel, and God was well aware of it. Cain had some real issues.

In 1 John 3:12 we read: "Not as Cain, who was of that wicked one, and slew his brother. And wherefore slew he him? Because his own works were evil, and his brother's righteous." Cain had an evil heart. No doubt, with this evil heart came some serious anger management issues. Notice Cain's response in Genesis 4:9 when God asked him where his brother was. He said, "Am I my brother's keeper?"

My response to Cain's question would have to be yes, because if you are not your brother's keeper, then quite possibly you're his killer.

Yes, Cain had some real issues, and they showed through clearly in his worship to God. That's why God wasn't pleased with his offering. Cain had a heart that had already rejected his brother. You can't reject your brother and expect God to receive, or be pleased with your worship.

Read what the Bible says in Matthew 5:23-24, *NASB*:

> Therefore if you are presenting your offering at the altar, and there remember that your brother has something against you, leave your offering there before the altar and go; first be reconciled to your brother, and then come and present your offering.

God doesn't want us to even attempt to bring our offering of praise and worship to His altar if there is need of reconciliation between us and our brother. There must be total and complete openness between us and God, as well as between one another.

Psalm 51:6, *NASB*, says, "Behold, You desire truth in the innermost being, and in the hidden part You will make me know wisdom."

God desires us to be truthful to our very core with Him, and with one another. That's the only way we can truly approach His presence. When we combine these two discussions on spirit and truth we get the following interpretation of John 4:24: "They that worship Him must connect with Him spiritually, with unbridled passion, holding nothing back, and be completely real, concealing nothing."

Let's venture a little deeper into the meanings of *spirit* and *truth* by using the story of the woman with the issue of blood in Mark 5. This woman had been sick for 12 long years with a hemorrhage that seemed incurable. Hoping to get well, she tried everything and spent all her money on doctors, but only got worse. However, when she heard about Jesus her *spirit* and *truth* moment came. Mark 5:27-28, *NASB*, says,

> After hearing about Jesus, she came up in the crowd behind Him and touched His cloak. For she thought, "If I just touch His garment, I will get well."

First this woman, who obviously knew about Jesus and His reputation, heard He was coming to town and believed He could help her. In other words, she acknowledged the deity of Jesus and His ability to heal her. Jesus said in John 4:24 that "God is a Spirit: and they that worship him must worship him in spirit and in truth." One way to worship God *in spirit* is to fully acknowledge and accept who His is; His unlimited power and ability to handle any issue man could ever have. There was no doubt in this woman's heart and mind that Jesus, the Son of God, could heal her. That is why, as she pressed through the crowd to reach Jesus, she had no inhibitions or fears. She was totally convinced that Jesus was THE ONLY answer for her sickness.

This brings us to the *truth* element in this story. Clearly, this woman was in very bad condition. Having suffered such a severe illness for so long, likely she even possessed an unpleasant body odor that caused her embarrassment. It's also likely that she felt unclean and like an outcast, much like the lepers of that day. However, none of that hindered her from pressing through the crowd to reach Jesus and touch His garment. She realized her sickness was not something she could manage—that she had no ability to heal herself. Everything she tried had failed miserably. If she didn't get to Jesus she would eventually die. This was the moment of *truth* for this woman, who fully acknowledged who she was not.

Until we are willing to acknowledge that we don't have the answer, and realize that without Him we can do nothing, our issues will continue to plague us. This woman was truthful with herself and with God. She was willing to fully expose her issue to connect with the Issue Healer, the only one Who could heal her.

If we are going to worship God *in truth*, we must be willing to do the same.

When we combine the *spirit* and *truth* displayed by this woman, we see that *spirit* means "to fully acknowledge who God is," and *truth* means "to fully acknowledge who you are not." When we are able to come to God with that level of humility and transparency, then we can also be healed of all our issues.

Another interesting thing to point out about John 4:23 is that Jesus said *true worshippers* will worship the Father. If there are true worshippers, then there must also be false worshipers. How do we distinguish a true worshipper from a false worshipper? Anyone who does not worship God in both spirit and in truth would have to be a false worshipper. My friend, we are not talking about people who do not know God. We are talking about people who come to church every Sunday but rarely, if ever, connect with God. They don't go after God with passion, breathing hard. Many others go to church with issues and hang-ups, but never expose them openly to God. They are like a person who invites you in to their home, but only allows you to go in to certain rooms. God desires to explore every room of our heart. Allowing Him to do this is the only way that we can become true worshippers.

Access Denied

They that worship God must look like Him. It's not true worship unless your spirit resembles God's Spirit. It's not true worship unless your image matches His image. Have you ever watched a movie or TV program where an employee of a highly secure company had to go through some type of identification scanner to gain access to their work area? It was usually some type of device that read their voice, eye, hand or fingerprint. Companies that deal with highly sensitive information do this because they want to make sure anyone who attempts to gain access is, in fact, authorized to be there. A company wants to make those attempting to gain access match the identity records that are on file. If an employee's print is recognized by the system as a match, then they gain access. But if there is no match in the system, access is denied.

Every time you worship God, your heart goes through a spiritual identification security checkpoint because God is looking to see if your heart matches His. Every time you come to church God is scanning your heart to see if your image and likeness matches His. If there is no match, access to His presence is denied, because they that worship Him "must" worship Him in spirit and truth (John 4:24). The only exception to this rule is those who come to God with a repentant heart, seeking forgiveness. Since they came with a repentant heart, God would never reject them. Now, once we come to God in repentance we must continue to grow in God—including in the area of worship. If we grow lax in our relationship with God, our heart can wax cold and our worship can become lifeless.

As we stated earlier, if there are true worshippers then that means there are false worshippers. Not everyone who is lifting their hands in praise and worship to God is gaining access to the throne room. I would venture to say that those who have lost their true heart for worship at some point were true worshippers. But the trials of life, along with the lies of the enemy, have caused them to lose sight of their true identity. But it only takes one precious moment of true surrender to get it back.

Some people are just going through the motions of worship to satisfy their religion. Access denied. Others think they're doing God a favor by offering their musical talents in church. Access denied. Some have not yet fully yielded their lives to God. Access denied. Many will say, "Lord, didn't I do this and that in Your Name?" But God's reply will be, "Access denied. I never knew you."

God Is Looking
The Bible says in John 4:23, "But the hour cometh, and now

is, when the true worshippers shall worship the Father in spirit and in truth: for the Father seeketh such to worship him." Read the last part of that verse: "For the Father seeketh such to worship him." What exactly is that saying? It's saying God is on the lookout for "true worshippers." He is always looking for someone who will worship Him in spirit and truth. He's not looking for false worshippers or nonchalant praisers. He's looking for desperate worshippers and praisers.

In Mark 5, beginning at verse 25, the story is told of a woman who was very sick. She had been hemorrhaging for 12 long years and had spent all her money on doctors who couldn't find a cure. She heard that Jesus was coming to town, so she made a last-ditch effort to be healed. She decided to try and get close enough to Jesus, believing if she touched the hem of His garment she would be healed. That passage in Mark 5 is a little long, but it's worth reading. Take a look at verses 25-34:

> And a certain woman, which had an issue of blood twelve years, and had suffered many things of many physicians, and had spent all that she had, and was nothing bettered, but rather grew worse, when she had heard of Jesus, came in the press behind, and touched his garment. For she said, If I may touch but his clothes, I shall be whole. And straightway the fountain of her blood was dried up; and she felt in *her* body that she was healed of that plague. And Jesus, immediately knowing in himself that virtue had gone out of him, turned him about in the press, and said, Who touched my clothes? And his disciples said unto him, Thou seest the multitude thronging thee, and sayest thou, Who touched me? And he looked round about to see her that had done this thing. But the woman fearing and trembling, knowing what was done in her, came and fell down before him, and told him all the truth. And he said unto her, Daughter, thy faith hath made thee whole; go in peace, and

be whole of thy plague.

This desperate woman pressed through the crowd as Jesus was passing by, and with what may have been her last bit of strength, stretched and reached for His garment. And with that one touch, desperate faith intersected with a willing Father, and this woman's life was changed forever. Instantly, she knew something had happened. And so did Jesus. A small dose of the power of Almighty God went from Jesus and into this woman's body, healing her instantly. Jesus, having felt the surge too, stopped and asked, "Who touched My clothes?" His disciples couldn't believe Jesus would ask this question, because the crowd was so thick with people bumping up against Him, trying to touch Him as He walked by. But this woman's touch was different than everybody else's.

I can almost picture Jesus in this huge crowd longing for somebody to touch Him in the right way. Someone to pull on His Divinity, to put a demand on His power. I can see Jesus looking around hoping that someone, anyone, would notice who He really was and reach out to Him in desperation. And in that moment, this one sick woman answered the bell.

This story is really an indictment on the Church. Think about it: Out of all the people who came to church that day, only one person touched Jesus in a way that got His attention. Only one person out of many was desperate. Everyone else was there with wrong motives. When you go to church this coming weekend, how many people sitting around you will be desperate? And how desperate will you be?

When was the last time you were really desperate for God to move in your life? When was the last time you stretched and reached for Him with everything within you? This story teaches us that God is looking for those who will worship Him in that manner. God is looking for passionate people who will make a joyful noise, and not be concerned about what others in the crowd might say. God is looking for someone who is not too dignified to lift their hands and give Him the praise He deserves. He's looking for someone who doesn't have to be coached or pleaded with to give Him praise.

You may not always feel like praising God, but He's still looking. Things may not be going exactly as you planned, but He's still looking. Your bank account may be a little low, but He's still looking. You might even be between jobs, but God is still looking. You may not be driving the car you desire, but He's still looking. You might be struggling with some habit or weakness right now, but He's still looking. You might be a little discouraged right now, but God is still looking.

That's why worship is so important—because God is always looking. Your worship is not predicated on your circumstances, but rather on God's greatness and goodness. And if He's good all the time, then we should worship Him all the time. God is looking to see how great you think He is. He's looking for someone to pay proper homage to Him. He's looking for His image. He's looking for someone who reminds Him of Himself. Realize that we were created in the image and likeness of God, and therefore we have no higher calling than to worship Him.

Are you a True Worshipper?

You are a True Worshipper if you worship God on His spiritual frequency. Praise and worship on an AM or FM frequency is just not going to cut it. It takes a "serious" spiritual satellite to connect with God. How do you get on God's frequency? Simple. You just ask Him. A yielded heart of complete obedience is all that is required.

You are a True Worshipper if you make it your quest to lay aside every weight and sin which so easily besets you, so that your worship is not encumbered by anything.

You are a True Worshipper if you never allow anything to hinder your praise. If someone talking about you stops your praise, you're not a true worshipper. If a broken relationship stops your worship, you're not a true worshipper. If getting fired from your job hinders your praise, you're not a true worshipper. If a low bank account puts your praise on empty, you're not a true worshipper.

You are a True Worshipper if you spend more time in God's presence than you do on Facebook or other social media.

You are a True Worshipper if you have this decree: "Nothing shall separate me from the love of God."

You are a True Worshipper if you can't wait to get to the house of God to express your love and devotion to Him.

You are a True Worshipper if you are glad when someone says to you, "Let's go to the house of the Lord."

You are a True Worshipper if you don't need any music to worship God.

You are a True Worshipper if you don't need to be in a church to worship God.

You are a True Worshipper if you don't need a worship leader to be able to worship God.

You are a True Worshipper if you never want to leave the presence of God. Like Joshua, you want to stay in the tent (Exodus 33:7).

What Is Praise?

We have already established that praise and worship is a matter of the heart and a life yielded to the Father. But what do praise and worship look like when expressed outwardly? First, it is important to understand there is a marked difference between expressions of praise and expressions of worship. Praise is an action word. We can easily derive this from the seven Hebrew words for praise we discussed in Chapter 3. Some of those words for praise include to shout, to clap, to wave the hands, to dance and even to act clamorously foolish. You really cannot praise God outwardly without engaging in some type of movement or action. Your love for God should show outwardly. Your excitement about God's goodness in your life should show outwardly. People at sports events aren't stiff and quiet. They are shouting, lifting their hands and even leaping for joy when their team is winning.

Guess what? If you are a servant of Almighty God, you are on the winning team, and you have something to be excited about. Don't be apprehensive in giving God your full expressions of praise in response to His goodness in your life.

Like at a sports event, praise is like a rallying cry. Praise has a way of joining hearts together for one cause. This is one of the things that differentiates praise from worship. Most of the time, when we sing praises we are talking about God to one another. We are reminding one another about the greatness of God. Yes, we are definitely praising Him, but most of our shouting, clapping and dancing is with each other about God. Just think about some of the praise songs you sing in your church. I would venture to say that with a great majority of them you are not singing directly to God, but rather to your neighbor in celebration about God.

Praise and worship, metaphorically speaking, can be compared to climbing a mountain. So, let's just say that when we engage in praise and worship to God, we are going on a journey up a mountain to ultimately meet with Him. Our destination is the top of the mountain, but we must start at the base.

In this scenario, praise is generally what happens at the base of the mountain. If you and I were going to be part of a group that went mountain climbing, we would first meet at the base of the mountain. We would get out of our cars and unload our gear. We would greet each other as we gathered, and probably make statements to each other like:

"Man, isn't this awesome!"

"I can't wait to get up there!"

"Have you climbed this mountain before?"

"I am so glad you are going. When you get to the top you are going to be blown away."

"I am so excited to be here."

We are talking to each other about the mountain. We're excited and energetic about the climb, and have a great anticipation for what awaits at the top. We begin the climb and continue to talk to each other because we are excited. That's what praise is like. We initially join together on Sunday morning and say things to one another like:

"Come into this house. Magnify the Lord."

"I am a friend of God."

"I'm trading my sorrows for the joy of the Lord."

"Let the glory of the Lord rise among us."

"Come, now is the time to worship."

"Shout to the Lord."

"Mighty is our God."

"I will call upon the Lord."

I realize there are many praise songs that speak directly to God, and we need more. However, for the most part, praise songs have typically been a rallying cry directed at one another as an encouragement and reminder of the greatness of God. This is a very joyous and exciting time, because we are beginning our ascent up the mountain to meet with our heavenly Father.

One of my all-time favorite television shows is *The Price is Right*. To me, this is reality TV at its very best. It is a show with real people expressing real emotions at the possibility of winning real prizes. This makes the outpouring of their exuberance and excitement genuinely authentic. I absolutely love watching this program, as I root for these everyday people who have a chance to win some really nice prizes.

So, what does this have to do with a discussion on the meaning of praise? Well, I think this show gives us a great picture of what praise is. The audience is so excited and exuberant over the possibility of having their name called. Can you imagine an entire congregation reacting like this in a church service? And it doesn't stop there. When a person's name is called, the fever pitch goes to even a higher level. The person who is selected jumps up with excitement, high-fiving people on their way to the front, as the audience goes crazy. Wouldn't this be a cool reaction in church during an invitation for salvation? When someone stands to give their life to Christ, the entire congregation leaps to their feet with exuberant praise as the new convert high-fives his way to the altar. It could happen.

Here's my point with this whole *The Price is Right* analogy: These people are excited to be on that show and they are showing it with reckless abandon. It's not quiet in that studio audience, and no one is just sitting there watching everyone else go crazy. That, my friend, is a great example of what praise is all about. And here's the funny thing about it: With all the excitement expressed on that show over someone being called to "Come on down!" at that particular point in the show nobody has won anything. They are screaming and going crazy simply over the possibility of winning a prize.

Compare that to us, God's children, who have already been given the prize of eternal life through Jesus Christ who set us free from our bondage of sin. So, why are we so apprehensive in our praise? We have already won the heavenly showcase!

What Is Worship?

Praise is important, because as we are climbing the mountain it gets us prepared or in the right frame of mind and spirit to encounter God. However, as we get close to the top of the mountain, things change. The presence of God is so overwhelming that our attention is no longer on our co-climbers, but on Him. We have now entered the realm of worship. We are no longer talking to one another, but rather talking directly to God, and saying things like:

"I worship You, Almighty God."
"Here I am to worship."
"There is none like You."

The word *worship*, used in John 4:23-24 is taken from the Greek word *proskuneo*, and has the following meaning: " *pros*: to go toward with the intent to touch or kiss"; "*kuneo*: like a dog licks its masters hand or feet."

When you put those two definitions together, it literally means, "to go toward with the intent to kiss, like a dog licks its master's hand."

A great example of this definition of worship is found in Luke 7:37-38, when a sinner woman comes to see Jesus.

> And there was a woman in the city who was a sinner; and when she learned that He was reclining at the table in the Pharisee's house, she brought an alabaster vial of perfume, and standing behind Him at His feet, weeping, she began to wet His feet with her tears, and kept wiping them with the hair of her head, and kissing His feet and anointing them with the perfume *(NASB)*.

What a great picture of worship displayed by this woman! She forgot about all those who were around her. She didn't care what it cost her in terms of perfume seemingly being wasted. The only thing that mattered was being in the presence of Jesus. Now, I am not saying that unless you kneel it is not considered worship. But what I am saying is that when you worship, no matter what your posture, there can be nothing more important to you than being in the presence of Jesus. Let me also say that the presence of God will oftentimes bring you to your knees, if not your face, and you need to be yielded enough to fully surrender in those moments. Many times our pride keeps us from tapping into deeper depths of worship that God desires us to experience with Him.

Let me give you one more visual example of worship.

Have you ever watched video footage of a mega-superstar like Elvis Presley or Michael Jackson in concert? Have you ever noticed some of the people in the audience, especially those close to the stage? Many of them are screaming the star's name with hands extended, begging for the star to touch them. Others are so overwhelmed with the gravity of the moment they just stand there and weep. And others literally pass out and have to be carried out by security. This is their mountaintop experience. These people were worshipping their idol. Just to be in the presence of their idol literally brought them to their knees.

While they were on their way to the concert, no doubt they were talking with their friends about how good a singer and dancer this performer is, and how they couldn't wait to get to the concert. They were talking to one another about the mega-star. This is praise. But once they get to the concert, actually in the presence of their superstar, they forget about their friends and are totally engrossed in what their idol is doing on stage. That is worship.

Yes, first and foremost, praise and worship is a godly lifestyle. It is who you are, not what you do. Yet, because praise and worship is who you are, it is what you love to do the most. Praise and worship is something that comes naturally, because expressing our love to God comes naturally. And know this, when you make the effort to go meet with God in praise and worship, He will come to meet with you.

Chapter 5
The Third Key

"Guard your steps when you go to the house of God. Go near to listen rather than to offer the sacrifice of fools, who do not know that they do wrong."
—**Ecclesiastes 5:1,** *NIV*

The phrase *praise and worship* is widely known around the world as that first part of a church service where we honor God through songs of, well…praise and worship. No doubt you have heard, and most probably used this phrase on occasion in one of these, or other forms: "What songs are we doing for praise and worship?" "Wow, praise and worship was awesome this morning!" "We have a new praise and worship leader."

In a great majority of Christian churches today, praise and worship, for the most part, involves the congregation expressing its love for God with the singing of a couple of praise songs and a couple of worship songs. While it is not in any way my intention to demean what we offer God in our services, I do believe there is something we are missing as it relates to this whole idea of praise and worship. There is no way God intended for that first 15 to 20 minutes of a service to be the extent of our mountaintop experience with Him. I submit to you that there is a third key that unlocks the door to a deeper level of intimacy with God far beyond praise and worship alone.

When we engage in praise and worship in a church service, and the last stanza of the last song is sung, have we gone as far as we can go? Have we gone as high as we can go? Have we gone as deep as we can go? At that moment, have we exhausted every possibility of connecting with the Father in the most effective way? Or have we just gone through the motions for the sake of religion?

As I said, I don't condemn or demean what we have become accustomed to offering God in our services. Exuberant praise is a great way to begin a service. It creates excitement within the service and joins hearts together. Praise is a rallying cry about our King. Worship is a great follow-up to praise, because it draws us closer to God, taking the focus off us and placing it more on Him. Worship helps settle us and reminds us that there really is nothing more important than being in God's presence. That said, I believe one of the greatest oversights in the Body of Christ is assuming that the praise and worship experience, as we understand it, is in and of itself complete.

The phrase *praise and worship* was mostly derived from Psalm 100:4, which says, "Enter His gates with thanksgiving and His courts with praise. Give thanks to Him, bless His name" *(NASB)*.

In this verse, the words *thanksgiving* and *praise* have somewhat interchangeable meanings. They both basically mean praise to God with thanksgiving, as well as a song or hymn of praise. Thanksgiving could be considered a little more exuberant, while praise in this verse is more of a subdued expression of worship. So, in a sense David was saying "Enter His gates with praise and His courts with worship." Hence, the term *praise and worship*. But as I mentioned earlier, we have a dilemma because praise and worship cannot represent the full extent of our intimacy with God. There has to be a third element, or dimension.

You see, anytime God wants to complete or seal something, He incorporates the number 3. Do you know how a piece of solid material becomes a solid? It's made up of three dimensions: length, width and height. That third element of height is also termed depth or thickness. A solid, by definition, is not a solid with just the first two dimensions of length and width. For it to become a solid you must incorporate depth, which is the dimension that looks downward, backward or inward. Without that third dimension of depth, the process of becoming a solid is incomplete.

Likewise, our worship experience with God is incomplete without a third dimension. Unless we can gain access to this place in the Spirit, our worship experience has no depth.

The number 3 is a perfect number. It is the number of completion. It symbolizes divine perfection, which points to the divine nature of God: the Father, the Son and the Holy Spirit. First John 5:7 says, "For there are three that bear record in heaven, the Father, the Word, and the Holy Ghost: and these three are one."

In addition to this three-part nature of God, there are His three-part characteristics, which are omniscient (all-knowing), omnipotent (all-powerful) and omnipresent (everywhere present at one time). God is complete. There is nothing about Him that is unfinished. This principle of three is intricately woven into who God is and how He operates in heaven and earth.

When God wants to complete something, He incorporates the number 3, because He wants to make it look as much like Himself as possible. He makes it in His image. That's how He completed us.

The Book of 3s

The Word of God is filled with evidence that proves the number 3 is God's number of completion. Here are just a few examples.

In Revelation 1:8: God describes Himself as He who is, He who was and He who is to come. In addition:

- God created man and gave him: 1. body; 2. soul; and 3. spirit.
- God gave man: 1. thoughts; 2. words; and 3. deeds; which represent the sum total of man's capabilities.
- God put man in time and gave him: 1. a past; 2. a present; and 3. a future; thus completing our time spent on earth.
- In Him we: 1. live; 2. move; and 3. have our being (Acts 17:28).
- All of mankind came from the three sons of Noah: Shem, Ham and Japheth.
- When God cut covenant with Abraham, He told him to get three animals: a heifer, a goat and a ram, each of which had to be 3 years old that. (Genesis 15:9).

- When Moses consecrated Aaron and his sons to the priesthood, he was instructed to kill a lamb and put the blood three places on their body: the tip of their right ear, the thumb of their right hand and the big toe of their right foot (Leviticus 8:23-24).
- There were three major feasts each year: the Feast of Passover, the Feast of Harvest and the Feast of Tabernacles.
- When Moses sent men to search the Promised Land, God sent the men back to Moses with three things: grapes, figs and pomegranates, proving to the children of Israel that this land was a sealed deal for them (Numbers 13:23).

This idea of 3 being the number of completion is further proven in the New Testament. Take a look:

- At Jesus' birth, the Wise Men brought three gifts: gold, frankincense and myrrh.
- On three different occasions Jesus was tempted by Satan, and each time Jesus responded by saying three words: "It is written."
- Jesus' public ministry began at age 30, which is a multiple of three; and it lasted three years.
- When Jesus fed the multitudes, He took the bread and did three things: 1. He blessed it, 2. He broke it, and 3. He gave it.
- There are only three recorded times of Jesus raising someone from the dead. Most notably was the calling of Lazarus out of a tomb by using just three words: "Lazarus, come forth!"
- Jesus calmed the raging sea by speaking three words: "Peace, be still."
- On the night He was betrayed, Jesus prayed three separate times in the garden of Gethsemane.
- Jesus was betrayed by Judas Iscariot for 30 pieces of silver.

- Peter denied knowing Jesus three times. Later, Jesus restored Peter three times.
- Jesus was crucified along with two other men, which meant a total of three men died on crosses.
- Jesus' last three words were: "It is finished."

But it doesn't stop there, because "3" is also the number of Resurrection.

- In Genesis 1, on the third day of Creation God resurrected the earth from the water.
- On the third day after Jonah was swallowed by a big fish, he was released from its belly.
- On the third day after Jesus' crucifixion, He rose from the dead, thus *solidifying*, *sealing* and *completing* our victory in Him!

Do you think all of this is just a huge coincidence? Not by any means. Nothing in God is finished or complete unless it incorporates His "three-key" process. So, here's my question: Why do most of our corporate church celebrations consist only of two keys: praise and worship? Where is the third key?

In the "praise and worship" scripture, Psalm 100:4, mentioned earlier, David was giving the people of his day a format for worship. In doing so, he also painted a very interesting picture of where specifically they were to worship. To understand this better you must have a basic understanding of the Tabernacle of which David spoke. There were three distinct sections to the Tabernacle. Isn't that interesting? Let me briefly discuss all three.

The Outer Courts

The Outer Courts was an enclosed yard surrounded by walls, with a gated entrance. This was the place of sacrifice for the children of Israel. It is interesting to note that this courtyard contained three things: the Brazen Altar for sacrificing animals; the Brazen Laver for washing the sacrifice; and the Bronze Platform from which the priest spoke. This courtyard served as the place that we would call our places of worship today. It is also symbolic of the initial work of the Holy Spirit, who came to draw man to God and remind or convict him of his sin. The Outer Courts was as close as the children of Israel could get to the Ark of the Covenant, where the presence of God dwelt, which was located in the Most Holy Place.

The Holy Place

The Holy Place was a room just outside the Most Holy Place. This room also had three pieces of furniture: the Seven-branch Golden Candlestick, which is symbolic of Jesus being the Light of the world; the Table of Showbread, which symbolizes Jesus being the Bread of Life; and the Golden Altar of Incense, which symbolizes Jesus being our advocate. The idea here is that Jesus, before His physical life, death and resurrection, was our go-between. He stood between the Outer Courts and the Most Holy Place and pleaded our cause before the Throne. While we were sacrificing for our sin outside in the Outer Courts, Jesus was our incense in the Holy Place, making sure the stench of our sin did not reach God's nostrils in the Most Holy Place. The priests would go into the Holy Place to light the candles, refresh the bread, and make sure incense burned continually.

The Most Holy Place

Separated from the Holy Place by a large floor-to-ceiling veil curtain, the Most Holy Place, also called the Holy of Holies, is where the manifest presence of God resided. In this room was one piece of furniture, the Ark of the Covenant. Inside the Ark there were three items: the Tablets of Stone, Aaron's Rod that budded, and the Golden Bowl of Manna. These three items in the Ark are symbolic of the Divine Nature of God as described in 1 John 5:7, "…these three are one." Only the High Priest could go into the Most Holy Place, and he only went in once a year to offer atonement for the children of Israel.

Now, with this layout of the tabernacle in mind, with its three sections, we can better understand what David was saying in Psalm 100:4: "Enter into his gates with thanksgiving, *and* into his courts with praise: be thankful unto him, and bless his name."

When he said, "Enter into his gates," he was speaking of the entrance or walkway leading into the Outer Courts. When David said, "and into his courts," he was talking about actually arriving in the courtyard where all the animals were sacrificed. David was instructing us to enter the gates with thankful praise to God for all His goodness.

Next, we were encouraged to enter the courts with a hymn. If we were living by this template of worship today, we would all get dressed for church on Sunday and then, as we drove to the church and pulled into the parking lot, we would start praising God. We would then get out of our cars and worship as we stood or knelt down in the parking lot. We would never go inside the sanctuary, which represents the Holy Place, and we would never go up on the platform of the church which, for this discussion, we can say represents the Most Holy Place.

We, the common folks, could never go any further than the Outer Courts, or the parking lot.

Again, this scripture in Psalm 100:4 has been widely accepted as the pattern for what we call praise and worship today. However, since we are under a New and Living Covenant, we can now go further than the Outer Courts. If this is the case, for God's process to be complete there has to be a third key that gives us access to a place beyond praise and worship.

The format for praise and worship which David wrote about in Psalm 100 was based on the restrictions of the Old Covenant. The common people were limited to the Outer Courts, the priests to the Holy Place, and the High Priest to the Most Holy Place once a year. But we now have a New Covenant. Through Jesus Christ defeating death, and the veil of the Temple being torn, we can now go all the way in to the Most Holy Place. After years and years of animal sacrifice, Jesus decided to be our sacrifice. He walked out of the Holy Place, went out to the Outer Courts and allowed Himself to be sacrificed once and for all, thus ending the need for animal sacrifices for the forgiveness of sin.

Hebrews 10:10-12, *NASB*, says, "By this will we have been sanctified through the offering of the body of Jesus Christ once for all. Every priest stands daily ministering and offering time after time the same sacrifices, which can never take away sins; but He, having offered one sacrifice for sins for all time, sat down at the right hand of God." When Jesus died on the cross of Calvary, it opened the *door* for us to go beyond the Outer Courts. In verses 19-22 we read: "Having therefore, brethren, boldness to enter into the holiest by the blood of Jesus, by a new and living way, which he hath consecrated for us, through the veil, that is to say, his flesh; and having an High priest over the house of God; Let us draw near with a true heart in full assurance of faith…."

> Let us therefore come boldly unto the throne of grace
> that we may obtain mercy, and find grace to help in
> time of need (Hebrews 4:16).

Sweet Communion

Under the New Covenant, we can now get closer. Jesus came to take us beyond the Outer Courts, past the Holy Place, and right into the Most Holy Place. Thank God we no longer have to stop in the parking lot. We are now free to go into the Holy of Holies and experience the presence of God on a level that would not have been possible without the way being opened for us by Jesus Christ.

So, what is the third key?

How do we complete or solidify our intimacy with God?

Praise, worship and what?

The answer is *communion*. Praise, worship and communion. That is God's process. Through Jesus Christ, we can enjoy sweet communion with our Heavenly Father.

In Exodus 25:10-22, God gives Moses specific instructions on how the Ark of the Covenant was to be built. Let's look at what God told Moses:

And they shall make an ark *of* shittim wood: two cubits and a half *shall be* the length thereof, and a cubit and a half the breadth thereof, and a cubit and a half the height thereof. And thou shalt overlay it with pure gold, within and without shalt thou overlay it, and shalt make upon it a crown of gold round about. And thou shalt cast four rings of gold for it, and put *them* in the four corners thereof; and two rings *shall be* in the one side of it, and two rings in the other side of it. And thou shalt make staves *of* shittim wood, and overlay them with gold. And thou shalt put the staves into the rings by the sides of the ark, that the ark may be borne with them. The staves shall be in the rings of the ark: they shall not be taken from it. And thou shalt put into the ark the testimony which I shall give thee. And thou shalt make a mercy seat *of* pure gold: two cubits and a half *shall be* the length thereof, and a cubit and a half the breadth thereof. And thou shalt make two cherubims *of* gold, *of* beaten work shalt thou make them, in the two ends of the mercy seat. And make one cherub on the one end, and the other cherub on the other end: *even* of the mercy seat shall ye make the cherubims on the two ends thereof. And the cherubims shall stretch forth *their* wings on high, covering the mercy seat with their wings, and their faces *shall look* one to another; toward the mercy seat shall the faces of the cherubims be. And thou shalt put the mercy seat above upon the ark; and in the ark thou shalt put the testimony that I shall give thee. And there I will meet with thee, and I will commune with thee from above the mercy seat, from between the two cherubims which *are* upon the ark of the testimony, of all *things* which I will give thee in commandment unto the children of Israel.

In verse 22, God ends His instructions to Moses by saying, "And there I will meet with thee, and I will commune with thee from above the mercy seat, from between the two cherubims which are upon the ark of the testimony, of all things which I will give thee in commandment unto the children of Israel." God said, "And there I will meet with thee." Where is "there"? In the Outer Courts? No. In the Holy Place? No. In the Most Holy Place? Yes! This is the third key. Communion with God is what completes, seals or solidifies our time with Him.

The word *communion* as used in the above verse, literally means, "to speak, to subdue, to answer, to appoint, to declare, to name, to promise, to teach, to give." God desires to speak to you, give you answers to vital questions, appoint you to a specific task, declare blessing over you, change your name, give you specific promises, teach you valuable lessons and much, much more. That's right; He wants to speak to you. But He won't do any of this in the Outer Courts or the Holy Place. It will only take place in the Most Holy Place. And if we don't take the time or opportunity to get there, or if we never take the time to listen, we will miss out on much of what He has for us. The sad truth is, we rarely do. We readily take the first two steps, because that's how we've been programmed, often stopping just short of the completion of God's process.

Remember, God said, "And there I will meet with thee...." Now, picture for a moment the Most Holy Place as being the very throne room of heaven. God is seated on His throne, and according to Hebrews 10:12, Jesus is seated at His right hand: "But this man, after he had offered one sacrifice for sins for ever, sat down on the right hand of God."

Picture God sitting on His throne, and Jesus sitting at His right hand. In John 6:35, Jesus said, "I am the bread of life: he that cometh to me shall never hunger; and he that believeth on me shall never thirst." And in Psalm 16:11, *NIV*, we read: "You will make known to me the path of life; you will fill me with joy in your presence, with eternal pleasures <u>at your right hand.</u>"

What do these verses tell us? They tell us that everything we could ever want or need can be found in the presence of God—at His right hand, IN Jesus. Our ultimate goal in this process we call praise and worship, is to get a clearer revelation of Jesus. When we get a clearer revelation of Jesus, we don't want for anything because He is our Shepherd. But this only happens when we unlock that third door of communion. When we commune with God, we truly feed from His table. John 6:35 intimates that we have a responsibility to come to Him in order to partake of His bread.

Jesus, who is at the right hand of God, is the bread we need to sustain us. He will feed us only if we take the time to eat.

I remember when I was a little boy, my mother would prepare dinner and tell me to come and eat. Initially, I would sit down and begin to eat. But if my mother left the room, I would get up from the table and dance around, watch TV and just get totally distracted from eating my dinner. My mother would eventually come back into the room and see me acting up. In a not-so-very-happy voice, she would say three things to me. I can almost hear her now:

"Alvin, shut up, sit down and eat!"

As harsh as that might sound, that's sometimes exactly what we need to do if we are going to discover the deeper things of God. We often come into His presence with little reverence, our own agenda and many words. We feel like we have to tell God everything, when in fact He already knows it all. While I know He cares about our complaints, disappointments, fears, what ifs and why Lords, we can never get an answer until we trust Him enough to shut up, sit down and eat.

Ecclesiastes 5:1, *NIV*, says, "Guard your steps when you go to the house of God. Go near to listen rather than to offer the sacrifice of fools, who do not know that they do wrong."

In reflecting on the process of going from praise to worship to communion, always keep in mind that the further we progress through each door of God's process, the less we should say. We typically say a whole lot during praise, and a little less during worship. However, communion should be a time when God does most of the talking. Communion is the time when we should be in a position of receiving instead of giving, listening instead of talking, knowing instead of wondering, eating instead of being distracted. We are truly missing out when we don't spend time eating from the hand of the Father.

> One thing have I desired of the Lord, that will I seek after; that I may dwell in the house of the Lord all the days of my life, to behold the beauty of the Lord, and to enquire in His temple (Psalm 27:4).

There is so much we do in our day-to-day lives that could be considered throwaways or distractions. In other words, if we didn't do them there would be no significant impact or effect on our lives either way. I heard a true story of a pastor who took deathly ill, and spent countless hours in a coma. When he came out of the coma, he said he had been in the presence of God. He said angels were visiting him in the hospital. He summed up this experience by making this statement: "You know, 90 percent of what we do on earth is not necessary." That is a bold statement, but when you've been in the manifest presence of God like this pastor has, your perspective on life can quickly change.

Maybe this is where David was coming from when he said, "One thing." David was saying that out of all the things I could be spending my time doing in this world, I only have one thing I truly have a passion for, and that is to be in the presence of God. Everything else pales in comparison to this one thing. I submit to you that the one thing can be summed up in one word: *communion*. Notice the last phrase in that verse says "to enquire in his temple." The word *enquire* simply means "to seek information." We go up to meet with God not just to feel good, but to seek information. We enter God's presence not so we can do all the talking, but to allow Him to speak to us. That's what communion is all about. We enquire of God, and then wait for Him to answer. We praise, we worship, and then we allow God to feed us from His table.

The problem is, we rarely slow down long enough to eat. But, you can't rush communion. Our fast-food, microwave mentality has conditioned us into thinking that if you can't get it quickly then just go on to something else. But that's not God's way of doing things. Jesus didn't even feed the multitudes until they first sat down in order. God will never speed up His process to fit your busy, disorganized schedule. Good things will always come to those who WAIT in His presence. That is the purpose of communion; to wait for Him. It is not a fast song, and it's not a slow song. As a matter of fact, it's not a song at all. It is *total surrender* at the feet of Jesus.

Read what Luke 10:38-42, *NIV,* says:

> As Jesus and his disciples were on their way, he came to a village where a woman named Martha opened her home to him. She had a sister called Mary, who sat at the Lord's feet listening to what he said. But Martha was distracted by all the preparations that had to be made. She came to him and asked, "Lord, don't you care that my sister has left me to do the work by myself? Tell her to help me!" "Martha, Martha," the Lord answered, "you are worried and upset about many things, but only one thing is needed. Mary has chosen what is better, and it will not be taken away from her.

What a great picture of communion. The ultimate goal is to be in the presence of God, and have Him speak to us. This was Mary's one driving passion. Like David in Psalm 27:4, this was her one thing: to sit at Jesus' feet and listen to Him speak. Jesus makes a very important distinction between serving Him and communing with Him. Martha served, but Mary communed. Jesus said that Mary chose what was better. This does not at all diminish the importance of servanthood. Jesus Himself said that if you want to be the greatest in the Kingdom you must first serve. However, if you are so busy serving that you don't have time to commune with God, like Martha, you are too busy; and you're missing the whole point of serving in ministry. Your effectiveness as a servant of God is directly proportional to your time spent at His feet in communion.

Luke 10:40 says Martha was distracted. I believe when Jesus responded to Martha by saying, "Martha, Martha," He was basically saying: "Martha, you just don't get it, do you?" Unfortunately, some of us just don't get it either. We have many things today that can and have distracted us from communing with God. We must choose what is best, and make sure that nothing is given more weight or importance than sitting at the feet of Jesus. Remember, communion is the third key that leads to deeper intimacy with God. It is the avenue through which everything is solidified, finished and completed. We should therefore never trade service for communion. God won't accept your service as a substitute for communion. We must take time daily to hear from God. This is our daily bread.

True and sweet communion takes place at the intersection of brokenness and complete surrender. And we can't get there on our own. We need the Holy Spirit to lead and guide us to that place. Second Corinthians 13:14 tells us: "The grace of the Lord Jesus Christ, and the love of God, and the communion of the Holy Ghost, be with you all. Amen." The primary function of the Holy Spirit is to bring us to that place of communion and fellowship with God. God sent the Holy Spirit to ensure that we could be with Him always! He instructed the Holy Spirit to help bring us to that place of surrender.

Most church services have great music ministries and awesome praise and worship. I'm sure many churches try to create moments of communion during service. But the fact is, we've become so time-conscious that there is rarely enough time during a weekend service to sit at the feet of the Father and listen to His words. Let me interject here that, as a pastor, I fully realize that the preached Word in a service is that time of communion with God, where He speaks through the pastor. So, I don't at all want to minimize the importance or effectiveness of God's servant speaking on His behalf.

That said, we're still just talking about one day out of the week. Is that the only time you're going to sit at the feet of Jesus and listen to His words? There are six more days during the week to have communion with God, so take advantage!

In Exodus 33:18, Moses prayed to God: "And he said, I beseech thee, show me thy glory." God's response came in verse 21: "Behold, there is a place by me, and thou shalt stand upon a rock:"

If I were Moses, my follow-up question would have been, "Lord, where is that place by You?" One of my frequent prayers is that I will find that place by Him. If I accomplish nothing else in this life, but I'm able to find that place by Him, my life will be complete. Noah found that place by God. He was a righteous and blameless man, who walked with God (Genesis 6:9). That's why Noah found favor in the sight of God. You need to make it your life's quest to find that place by Him. If you haven't discovered it yet, you're living well beneath your Kingdom privileges. And here's just a small piece of advice: You're going to have to dig a little deeper than 20 minutes of praise and worship on the weekend in order to find it.

Give Us This Day

In Exodus 16, *NASB*, God provided daily sustenance for the children of Israel with manna from heaven. Verse 4 says, "Then the Lord said to Moses, Behold, I will rain bread from heaven for you; and the people shall go out and gather a day's portion every day, that I may test them, whether or not they will walk in My instruction."

The word *bread* used here means "provision, sustenance, the word, wisdom, promise, direction, revelation, interpretation and truth." Everything the children of Israel needed to sustain them was provided in the manna. All they had to do was to follow God's instructions and gather their daily provision.

Remember, the bread or manna represents that which you

can only receive in the Most Holy Place, because God said in Exodus 25:22, *NKJV,* "There I will meet with you." You can only receive the bread of Life in the very presence of God. You can only receive this heavenly bread by using that third key of communion with the Father. Your daily prayer and cry to the Lord should be, "Lord, give me this day my daily bread." You don't receive manna in the Outer Courts. You don't receive manna in the Holy Place. You can only receive manna, and all that it represents, in the Most Holy Place.

We can't compromise, sacrifice or replace our manna with anything else. There are no shortcuts or substitutions for the daily bread that God provides for us. After all, why do we worship God? We worship Him because He deserves all the honor and praise we can give Him, and more. We worship Him because we love Him. But we also worship Him to have Him speak to us, because that's the only way we can become more like Him. The ultimate goal is to have God speak to us. We need God to speak to us. We cannot live without His manna.

We sometimes go to the doctor's office to have them tell us what is wrong with us. Doctors are educated and trained to diagnose our symptoms and give us their expert opinions. Yes, we tell the doctor what our symptoms are, what hurts and where it hurts. But at some point we have to stop talking and allow the doctor to tell us what the root of the problem is and the best possible treatment to overcome it.

In the same way, we need to allow Dr. God to speak to us daily and give us the instruction, wisdom and answers that will make us better, stronger and more like Him. He can't talk to us as long as we are talking. So, after we have prayed and cast our cares on Him, we need to be silent and allow God to give us our daily bread. That, my friend, is the pinnacle of our mountaintop experience in God's presence.

When I See the Worship

It is important that we don't see worship as something that is only expressed in church. As a matter of fact, the early Church many times met in homes. Experiencing the presence of God in your home is just as important as experiencing Him in church. I see the gathering of people together at a central location to worship God, as an extension of what takes place in the individual homes. It is the coming together of individual families to celebrate what has taken place separately during the week. The real purpose of church is to put into practice corporately what has been taking place all week in our individual homes. I have always felt that a church is made up of individual families, and if families are messed up then the church is not going to be that much better. We can strengthen the infrastructure of our churches if we understand that the presence of God is the missing link in our homes that can make this happen.

The presence of God in your home can and will make a big difference in your life. Just ask Obededom. In 2 Samuel 6, after David's first attempt to bring back the Ark of the Covenant failed, he ordered the Ark to be placed in the home of Obededom. Now remember, the Ark of the Covenant represented the very presence of God. So, one day Obededom gets a knock on the door and it's the newly appointed King David with his entire parade of people. David asks Obededom if they can keep the Ark in his house while they figure out why God killed someone who reached out to touch it. I'm sure Obededom could have responded by saying, "Uh, you want me to keep something in my house that has already killed somebody?" Truth is, Obededom probably didn't have a choice, seeing that it was the king who was making the request.

So David's people bring the Ark, the very presence of God, into Obededom's house, and then the king and his entourage leave. I can see Obededom and his family standing around the Ark and looking at it. The very presence of God is now in their home. Second Samuel 6:11 tells us what happened as a result.

> And the ark of the Lord continued in the house of Obededom the Gittite three months: and the Lord blessed Obededom, and all his household.

This same event is mentioned in 1 Chronicles 13:14: "And the ark of God remained with the family of Obededom in his house three months. And the Lord blessed the house of Obededom, and all that he had."

We don't really know what Obededom's economic status was prior to the Ark being brought into his house. One thing we do know is that whatever his status was prior to this event, it drastically improved in just three months' time. It improved so much that word got all the way back to David, who eventually came and removed the Ark from Obededom's house and returned the presence of God back to Jerusalem.

Listen, I'm not promising that you'll have an Obededom-like turnaround in your life if you make a concerted effort to bring the presence of God into your home. What I am saying is that when the presence of God is in your home, your entire household will be blessed, because wherever God is, His blessings are present as well.

It's time we get back to things like family prayer and family Bible study. It's time that we once again come together as families and acknowledge God in our homes. It's time we no longer allow the enemy to have our homes while we go to church.

Just before the children of Israel were delivered out of Egypt, God sent 10 plagues on Egypt to soften Pharaoh's heart. In the last plague, God sent a death angel to kill all the firstborn in Egypt. It's important to understand that the children of

Israel were only immune from this plague "if" they did exactly what God said. Exodus 11 and 12 tell us exactly what God required the children of Israel to do to save their firstborn from the death angel. In short, they were to take a young lamb, kill it and eat it in the evening. This was their form of worship in their home. They were then instructed to take the blood from the lamb and paint some of it outside on the doorposts and lintel, which was most probably the horizontal cross section above the entrance of the house.

God said to them that the death angel would come to each house, and when God saw the blood, the death angel would pass over that house. Understand that what God was asking them to do in terms of the animal sacrifice was not new to them. Again, this was the Israelites' form of worship. The blood on the doorposts and lintel was a sign to God that they had worshipped in their home. God was saying to them, "My children, things are going to get a little crazy tonight, but don't worry. Just worship Me. And when I see the worship, the evil will pass over your home."

That night, God came looking for worship. When He saw it, that house was saved from the destruction of the enemy.

The world is filled with all kinds of evil, but we can make our homes safe havens of God's presence. It doesn't mean the enemy won't come and try to get in. But he won't be able to stay long once he realizes that your home is a place where the presence of God dwells. In addition, the Bible says we are the temple of God. We are the house that God is coming to, hoping to see worship.

First Peter 2:5, *NASB*, says, "You also, as living stones, are being built up as a spiritual house…to offer up spiritual sacrifices acceptable to God through Jesus Christ." This gives new meaning to the powerful declaration Joshua made when he declared, "As for me and my house, we will serve the Lord" (Joshua 24:15). He was speaking of his entire household, but this can also apply to you as an individual: your body as the tabernacle of God. In fact, take a moment right now and place your hand on your heart and declare for your life and the lives of your family members what Joshua declared. Go ahead, say it: "As for me and my house, we will serve the Lord!"

There is power, strength and protection as we welcome the presence of God into our actual homes and spiritual homes. Friend, never forget that God is looking. And when He sees your worship, He will protect and bless your life beyond measure.

Chapter 6
Let's Bring the Presence Back

"And he said, My presence shall go with thee, and I will give thee rest."
—**Exodus 33:14**

When David became king of Israel, one of the first things he did was bring the Ark of the Covenant back to Jerusalem. We have already established in previous chapters that the Ark of Covenant represented the very presence of God amongst Israel. So, it appears David's No. 1 priority as the newly crowned king was to organize the return of the presence of God back to its rightful place in Jerusalem. In 1 Chronicles 13:3, during one of his first speeches as king, David rallied the people to get behind this most important project when he said, "Let us bring the ark of our God back to us, for we did not inquire of it during the reign of Saul" *(NIV)*.

Can you sense the passion and excitement in David's words to Israel? We know from the many psalms David penned that he had a love and appreciation for the presence of God that was beyond the norm. I have a feeling that, as king of Israel, this was something that had been stirring in David for quite some time.

Have you ever thought something like, *Man, if I ever became president of the United States, the first thing I would do is…?* David must have had this type of conversation with himself, because it doesn't seem like it took any time at all for him to jump right on this project. This is definitely something he had thought about extensively. He already knew how long the presence of God had been gone. That's why he was able to remind the people that they had been without God's presence during the entire time of King Saul's reign.

Perhaps in David's mind King Saul had dropped the ball by

allowing the presence of God to be taken from Jerusalem. Maybe David felt like things for the nation of Israel had pretty much gone downhill ever since that day when the presence of God was taken. I can almost hear David saying, "If I ever become king, the first thing I'm going to do is bring back the presence of God to Jerusalem." Maybe God heard it, too. Maybe this is one of the reasons God described David as a man after His own heart. It has always been God's heart for His people to exist and thrive under the shadow and covering of His presence.

The writer of Psalm 33 is unknown. However, it is widely believed that David wrote this psalm because he wrote the psalms that preceded and followed it. Seeing that David's first act as king was to bring the presence of God back to Jerusalem, it stands to reason that he would have written these words from Psalm 33:12:

> Blessed is the nation whose God is the Lord; and the people whom he hath chosen for his own inheritance.

David understood that the success of a nation hinges on whom that nation acknowledges and worships as God. It is an awesome thing to read that a newly elected government official actually got an entire nation back on the right spiritual footing immediately after taking office. Sad to say, nothing like that has happened in our lifetime. Most of our elected officials are too busy trying to be politically correct, trying to please everybody and not offend anyone in hopes of staying in office. But David didn't care about any of that. He didn't have a political agenda. All he knew was that if Israel was going to be successful as a nation, the presence of God had to be the centerpiece. David must have taught this truth to his son Solomon, who wrote in Proverbs 14:34, "Righteousness exalteth a nation: but sin is a reproach to any people."

My prayer is that God will once again raise up a man or woman "after His own heart" who, like David, will understand the importance of having God as the central focus of everything that is pursued and accomplished as a nation. As I read about the spiritual history of the United States, I see that there were some men who tried to keep our country on the right spiritual footing. For example, John Adams (March 1798) and Abraham Lincoln (March 1863) signed proclamations appointing a Day of National Humiliation, Fasting, and Prayer. It was these early proclamations that paved the way for the National Day of Prayer, which our nation now observes in May of each year. Unfortunately, our National Day of Prayer is far removed from the heart of what our forefathers desired in terms of a national day of spiritual observance. The main reason is that today, people are free to pray to whatever "god" they desire. So, the One and True God is lumped in with every other god, which means our National Day of Prayer is one of the most spiritually segregated days in our country, with no real spiritual benefit to our nation as a whole.

I've taken time to include Abraham Lincoln's 1863 proclamation here because I believe it to be a real eye-opener. As you read it, take a moment to reflect on the condition of our nation, and where we could be as a country if the truths expressed in this writing were widely held and followed by our politicians today. I have bolded certain statements for purpose of emphasis.

Proclamation 97—Appointing a Day of National Humiliation, Fasting, and Prayer—*March 30, 1863*

Whereas the Senate of the United States, **devoutly recognizing the supreme authority and just government of Almighty God in all the affairs of men and of nations**, has by a resolution requested the President to designate and set apart a day for national prayer and humiliation; and

Whereas **it is the duty of nations as well as of men to own their dependence upon the overruling pow-**

er of God, to confess their sins and transgressions in humble sorrow, yet with assured hope that **genuine repentance will lead to mercy and pardon**, and to recognize the sublime truth, announced in the Holy Scriptures and proven by all history, that **those nations only are blessed whose God is the Lord**;

And, insomuch as we know that by His divine law nations, like individuals, are subjected to punishments and chastisements in this world, **may we not justly fear that the awful calamity of civil war which now desolates the land may be but a punishment inflicted upon us for our presumptuous sins**, to the needful end of our national reformation as a whole people? We have been the recipients of the choicest bounties of Heaven; we have been preserved these many years in peace and prosperity; we have grown in numbers, wealth, and power as no other nation has ever grown. But **we have forgotten God.** We have forgotten the gracious hand which preserved us in peace and multiplied and enriched and strengthened us, and **we have vainly imagined, in the deceitfulness of our hearts, that all these blessings were produced by some superior wisdom and virtue of our own.** Intoxicated with unbroken success, we have become too self-sufficient to feel the necessity of redeeming and preserving grace, too proud to pray to the God that made us.

It behooves us, then, to humble ourselves before the offended Power, to confess our national sins, and to pray for clemency and forgiveness.

Now, therefore, in compliance with the request, and

fully concurring in the views of the Senate, I do by this my proclamation designate and set apart Thursday, the 30th day of April, 1863, as a day of national humiliation, fasting, and prayer. And I do hereby request all the people to abstain on that day from their ordinary secular pursuits, and to unite at their several places of public worship and their respective homes in keeping the day holy to the Lord and devoted to the humble discharge of the religious duties proper to that solemn occasion.

All this being done in sincerity and truth, let us then rest humbly in the hope authorized by the divine teachings that the united cry of the nation will be heard on high and answered with blessings no less than the pardon of our national sins and the restoration of our now divided and suffering country to its former happy condition of unity and peace. In witness whereof I have hereunto set my hand and caused the seal of the United States to be affixed.

Done at the city of Washington, this 30th day of March, A. D. 1863, and of the Independence of the United States the eighty-seventh.

ABRAHAM LINCOLN.
By the President

What makes the words of this proclamation so impactful is the fact that they still apply to the current condition of our country today. The truth is, we need more than just one day a year of humiliation, fasting and prayer as a country. We need an entire year or more! It's time to bring the presence of God back to its rightful place as the supreme power and authority that guides all that we do as a country. David said in 1 Chronicles 13:3 that the entire nation of Israel didn't enquire or acknowledge God for the entire time that Saul was in office. How many presidential terms have passed in the United States without America putting God first? How long has the presence of God been absent from our country?

It took just one man, David, whose passion for God's presence changed the course of an entire nation. All God needs is one person with reckless abandon. It's usually not an army that initiates change, but rather one, or a few who have the ability to ignite the hearts of many. God is looking for just one yielded heart, someone who doesn't care what others may think. He's looking for just one person of passion who, at all costs, is willing to bring honor to God in the proper way. He's looking for just one person who understands that before you can touch the world you have to see the value in connecting with your Creator.

Remember the woman with the issue of blood in Mark 5? This woman put her reputation on the line in order to connect with Jesus. Like this woman, our nation and world has some serious issues. We're bleeding and we don't even realize it. Until we bring the presence of God back and reconnect with Him, we will continue to suffer the effects of a nation and world that are no longer under the lordship of Christ.

The fact that the Ark of the Covenant had to be brought back to Jerusalem is an indictment on the people of that day. The fact that the presence of God had to be brought back means that somehow, it had been removed. Who let that happen? What specific decisions were made that led to this? What series of events or votes or amendments were passed that allowed the presence of God to be removed from Israel? What had they done to allow the presence of God to be removed from their nation? We know, based on David's words, that Israel had neglected the presence of God and had stopped relying on His ability to lead and guide them as a country. What have we done as a country to push God into a small corner of our existence? What laws were passed? Who was more concerned with their political career or reputation than with standing up for God's presence? The list is too long.

I don't know about you, but as I look over the landscape of our country, it appears we have some serious and very troubling issues that continue to threaten the integrity of what our Founding Fathers desired our great country to be. Over the years, we have slowly chipped away at the spiritual foundation on which our nation was built. We've taken prayer out of our schools and replaced it with a loosely observed moment of silence. We allow the killing of innocent unborn babies. We have accepted and legally authenticated same-sex marriage. All these decisions are in direct violation of godly principles.

These, and other decisions over the years, have slowly eroded the moral fiber of our country, rendering the United States spiritually anemic. What is the result of our nation turning its back on God? A spirit of violence and destruction has been unleashed on our country, resulting in shootings in schools, malls, movie theaters and the like. Our moral standards are almost nonexistent, our family unit is confusing, there are major economic issues, and there is an increase in natural disasters, floods, tornadoes and hurricanes. While crime is at an all-time high, God is standing by, asking, "Can you hear Me now?"

In the midst of all this, the Church has no right to point its finger at the world. In many ways, we have failed to keep up our end of the spiritual contract. Before we can begin to speak to other nations about their issues, we have to first deal with our own. In short, we have left our first love (Revelation 2:4). We have become too complacent, too safe, too comfortable and too concerned with making church convenient and palatable for the people rather than pleasing to God.

We're trying to be sensitive to everyone except the King of kings.

In many cases, we have literally programmed the presence of God right out of our services.

Now listen, I get it.

I understand the reason behind some of the innovative changes that we have made over the years in how we approach "church." But my fear is that we have become so intoxicated with church growth that we have neglected the very purpose for which we gather.

We're too comfortable with our church valet parking, coffee bars, 10-minute worship, 20-minute sermons and no manifestation of the presence and power of God. We have treated the presence of God like an unwanted stepchild. It's time to bring back the presence of God! We must be like Moses, who refused to go another step without the presence of God. He said in Exodus 33:15, *NASB*, "[Lord,] if Your presence does not go with us, do not lead us up from here."

The problem with the Body of Christ is that we have been willing to journey on with our agendas and programs, not realizing that the presence of God was not even with us. Look at the last 30-plus years. In the '70s it was the "charismatic movement." In the '80s and early '90s it was "the Word" movement. In the mid-'90s to the present it has been the "seeker sensitive" movement. And with each movement there has been less and less of the presence of God experienced in our services. But it's time to bring the presence back!

How far are we willing to go without the presence of God? How far off target are we willing to go? I'm not willing to go any further. I'm like Moses; I'm not willing to go any further unless the presence of God goes with us. We don't need another Church movement, unless it's saturated with God's presence. Anything else is a waste of time.

In many ways, we fit what the Scripture says in Revelation 2:4. We have left our first love. We have become what Paul described in 2 Timothy 3:5, *NASB*, as a people who are "holding to a form of godliness, although they have denied its power." Paul went on to say, "They will not make any further progress." We are not progressing as a Church because we have forgotten God. We have not progressed as a nation because we have forgotten God. Instead, we have given valuable territory and license to the enemy to wreak havoc in our country.

True change can only come by first acknowledging the true change maker—Jesus Christ. God stands in the midst of a confused and disoriented America and world, desperate for relief, and His thoughts echo the famous words inscribed on the Statue of Liberty: "Give me your tired, your poor, your huddled masses yearning to breathe free."

But God says it in a different way. He says, "Come unto me, all ye that labour and are heavy laden, and I will give you rest" (Matthew 11:28).

Notice in 2 Samuel 7:1, *NIV*, what happened after David brought the presence of God back to its rightful place: "The Lord had given him rest from all his enemies around him." The nation of Israel could not experience rest until the presence of God was brought back to its rightful place.

America will never experience change, we will never experience true rest, and we will never be able to breathe freely again until we are willing to join together—red, yellow, black, white—and bring back the presence of God. As the songwriter wrote, "This is the air I breathe; Your holy presence living in me."

I pray that, like David, you will have the fearless heart of a true worshipper; that you will have the courage and tenacity to kill the lions that try to steal your praise, kill the bears that try to capture your worship, and slay the giants who try to interrupt your communion with God. I pray that you will always have the boldness to refuse to journey on without the presence of God as the centerpiece of your life, and may you always be willing to use The Third Key of communion to experience a deeper level of intimacy with the Father.

www.ingramcontent.com/pod-product-compliance
Lightning Source LLC
Chambersburg PA
CBHW070543300426
44113CB00011B/1779